C000276956

TALES FROM THE TWILIGHT ZONE

Most people have at least one strange story to tell – and some seem to go through life experiencing one weird event after another. While social scientists have put forward the idea of 'fantasy-prone individuals' in an attempt to explain – or explain away – stories of alien abductions or meetings with otherworldly entities, this doesn't begin to account for the fact that otherwise sane and level-headed people sometimes report the most bizarre experiences, and are usually left baffled, and sometimes rather unnerved, by their close encounters with the unexplained.

One of the problems faced by UFO witnesses, residents of haunted houses or families under siege from noisy poltergeists or mischievous 'little people' is just who to tell – at best, their stories might be greeted with incredulous laughter, while, at worst, they might be thought quite mad.

For 36 years, the letters pages of *Fortean Times* – and, more recently, its online forums – have been a haven for all those with strange tales to tell, a place where the oddest yarns will be listened to attentively, shared and compared in a communal effort to try and get to grips with the outer limits of the human condition.

This second volume of *It Happened to Me!* contains a selection of some of our favourite letters, dealing with everything from terrifying hauntings, demonic dogs and vanishing people to more benign oddities, like mysterious appearances of money or what might be termed 'guardian angels' offering help or advice.

So, if you want to be spooked, amazed or just plain perplexed – read on. And remember – when something strange happens to you, we'd love to hear about it.

David Sutton, Editor *Fortean Times*

It Happened To Me!

REAL-LIFE TALES OF THE PARANORMAL
VOLUME 2

Ordinary people's extraordinary stories from
the pages of **FORTEAN TIMES**

EDITED AND COMPILED BY
Paul Sieveking

PHOTOGRAPHY AND DESIGN
Etienne Gilfillan

EDITOR IN CHIEF
David Sutton

COVER IMAGE
Etienne Gilfillan

CROW IMAGE BY V PANDIYAN

PUBLISHING & MARKETING
Russell Blackman
020 7907 6488
russell_blackman@dennis.co.uk

BOOKAZINE MANAGER
Dharmesh Mistry
020 7907 6100
dharmesh_mistry@dennis.co.uk

IT HAPPENED TO ME! VOLUME 2 is published
by Dennis Publishing Ltd, 30 Cleveland Street,
London W1T 4JD. Company registered in England.
The "Magbook" brand is a trademark of Dennis
Publishing Ltd. All material © Dennis Publishing Ltd,
licensed by Felden 2009, and may not be reproduced
in any form without the consent of the publishers.
It Happened to Me Volume 2 ISBN 1-906372-94-2
All material copyright 2009.
Printed at Stones the Printers Limited

LICENSING
To license this product, contact Winnie Liesenfeld,
Publishing Services Manager:
020 7907 6134
winnie_liesenfeld@dennis.co.uk

DENNIS PUBLISHING LTD
DIGITAL PRODUCTION MANAGER: Nicky Baker
PRODUCTION DIRECTOR: Robin Ryan
MANAGING DIRECTOR OF ADVERTISING:
Julian Lloyd-Evans
NEWSTRADE DIRECTOR: Martin Belson

CHIEF OPERATING OFFICER: Brett Reynolds
GROUP FINANCE DIRECTOR: Ian Leggett
CHIEF EXECUTIVE: James Tye
CHAIRMAN: Felix Dennis

HOW TO CONTACT US
MAIL: 30 Cleveland Street, London W1T 4JD
PHONE: 020 7907 6000
EMAIL AND WEB
Website: www.forteantimes.com

To contact advertising:
James Clements 020 7907 6724
james_clements@dennis.co.uk

Change your address, open or renew a subscription
or report any problems at www.subsinfo.co.uk
0844 844 0049

It Happened To Me!

REAL-LIFE TALES OF THE PARANORMAL
VOLUME TWO

ORDINARY PEOPLE'S EXTRAORDINARY
STORIES FROM THE PAGES OF FORTEAN TIMES

CONTENTS

1 *Mysterious Helpers*

A visit from a mysterious and untraceable vet in Somerset... a wonderful yet unfindable restaurant in Iran... Stories like these have the feel of classic fairy tales, though like everything between these covers they are claimed by our correspondents to be sober truth. Then there are tales of vital aid in circumstances of imminent danger – could these be the interventions of guardian angels?

FROM OTHER DIMENSIONS?

EERIE HOUSE CALL

In 1962, I stayed for several months in one of the narrow Georgian houses on Bathwick Hill on the outskirts of Bath. My husband, my daughter and two rather noisy dachshunds were also in the house, but nevertheless I often felt uneasy.

One cold November morning soon after Guy Fawkes' Night, my dog Rudi suffered a virulent stomach upset. His companion, Liese, was unaffected, but Rudi grew noticeably worse and I obtained the number of the nearest vet from Directory Enquiries. The vets' receptionist told me that a number of dogs in the area were being effected by some form of epidemic, but though every surgery was jammed she thought it might be possible to arrange a visit.

It was 7.30 and very misty when the vet arrived – an extraordinarily pale young man, tall, slightly built and somewhat taciturn – indeed, curt to the point of rudeness. He placed Rudi on the table in the basement kitchen and the dog stopped whimpering almost immediately.

After a minute or two, the vet lifted him down and, taking a small box from his, bag broke his silence to tell me that the tablets it contained were to be taken every four hours. He said that the dog had developed a particularly nasty form of gastric upset, and for 48 hours he must be given no solid food. He would, however, recover if he took all the tablets. Considerably relieved, I tried to make light conversation as we went back upstairs, but he offered no response. As he went out into the foggy night, he didn't even say goodbye.

The tablets worked well, and within a matter of hours Rudi was himself again. The following morning, I rang the vet with the good news. The receptionist said the epidemic was very much worse; she was sorry no one had yet been able to look at my dog, but someone would be calling later in the day. I told her a vet had already been, but she insisted I must be mistaken. Their Mr X, Mr Y and Mr Z had all been occupied in other directions; but she promised to check. She soon called back to confirm that no one from the practice had called at a house on Bathwick Hill at any time in the previous week.

I contacted Directory Enquiries and by luck reached the same woman I had spoken to the day before. She remembered giving me the number – just that one number – but suggested that with such a mystery it would be worth checking other vets. She assembled a list of every vet for miles around, which I double-checked with a borrowed copy of Yellow Pages. I rang them all, and drew a blank.

Rudi made a full and speedy recovery. What the tablets were I never found out, but at least they were tangible and extraordinarily effective. The young man had left without mentioning payment and I assumed I would receive a bill, but while we remained in that house – for a further three months – no bill arrived.

Perhaps the vet was visiting from another dimension; or maybe he was one of those people, frequently medical practitioners, who are said sometimes to be whisked through space, without their knowledge, to render help where it's needed. We'll probably never know – unless there's an ageing veterinary surgeon who recalls mislaying half an hour of his life one November evening 37 years ago.

Ida Pollock, Lanreath-by-Looe, Cornwall, 1999

THE PHANTOM DINER

Some years ago, I was working as a civil engineer in Iran. In about 1956, 1 had to make a visit to Manjil in the north-west in connection with the construction of a cement factory, and went up there with an Iranian engineer. Manjil, the centre of a disastrous earthquake in the early 1990s, is on the road to Rasht, and about 150 miles (240km) from Tehran. At the time of my visit, it was very isolated and all that we had been able to eat was some unleavened bread and *dugh*, a type of liquid yogurt.

> ❝ *Some of these were occupied by drivers who were drawing on a hubble-bubble* ❞

We were in consequence very hungry as we drove back to Tehran. From time to time we met a lorry and would slither past each other. We were fortunate to be travelling in the summer, as the road was quite often impassable with snow in the winter. Eventually, we reached a plateau and, as we were still 120 miles (190km) from Tehran and 50 miles (80km) from Qazvin, the nearest town, any hope of eating was remote.

"Nothing much we can do," I said, "unless we can find a *tchae-khana*." This was the equivalent of a road-side café, where we were unlikely to get anything more substantial than a glass of weak tea, strained through a lump of sugar held between the teeth.

Just then, we came to a village with some single-storey mud huts, permanently dusty from the continual passage of lorries and cars, and with a very distinct and unmistakable landmark in the shape of a pile of rocks with one balanced precariously on top.

"Looks promising", I said to my Iranian companion as we pulled up behind some lorries. "Should get some tea at any rate." We got out of the car and walked through some scattering, squawking chickens to the long, low building in front of us. After the brilliant sun that had been shining on us all the way from Manjil, it took us some time to get accustomed to the gloom; but how wonderfully cool it was! Round the walls were rows of charpoys, those essentially functional beds made from rope and wood. Some of these were occupied by drivers who were drawing sporadically on a hubble-bubble. There were a few carpets and in the middle some chairs and rough wooden tables. The walls were bare, apart from a highly stylistic picture of Hussein the Martyr.

From the back, the proprietor hurried up. "Good afternoon," he said nervously, but in flawless English. "My name is Hovanessian... Armenian of course and," he added with a touch of pride, "my wife is a White Russian. What can I get for you?"

"My friend and I are very hungry", I answered. "We've had nothing to eat all day. Perhaps you can help us."

The Armenian smiled. "It is not often we have ferenguays... excuse me, I mean foreigners here," he said, "and it will be a great privilege and honour to prepare a meal for you. My wife and I are not unaccomplished as cooks. Please leave it to us." He ushered us to one of the wooden tables and swept imaginary dust away.

After a while, a beaming, moon-faced woman came in with a tablecloth and some cutlery, which she laid out very carefully. The lorry drivers examined us incuriously and the gurgle of the hubble-bubble echoed rhythmically as the stem was passed from one cupped hand to the next.

Presently, Mr Hovanessian came in himself with two bowls of soup. And what soup! The basic ingredients were cucumber, raisins and yogurt, served ice cold. I don't know what else had been added, but it was quite the most delicious soup I had ever tasted.

When we had finished, Mr Hovanessian asked me confidentially if I would like some wine. "We have two types", he said, "Rezayeh or Qazvin." I chose the red Qazvin and we drank it very cold. The next course was dolmas (stuffed vine leaves), which were delicious with a delicate flavour all their own. I asked for the recipe, but Mr Hovanessian was politely vague. "Oh, just vine leaves... rice, that from Rasht is particularly good... some meat and onions and a few herbs. This is not really an Iranian dish", he added, as if to justify his reticence.

The next course was Chelo Kebab, which I suppose can be called the national dish of Iran. Prior to grilling, the meat is marinated overnight in a special mixture of yogurt and spices. The Chelo part is rice prepared in butter so that a brown crust forms on top.

We ate in silence, almost with an air of reverence, and finished the meal with Turkish coffee drunk in a glow of contentment. The atmosphere was hazy, almost unreal. At last we felt it was time to go. I asked Mr Hovanessian how much we owed. He told us shyly and the price was astonishingly cheap. "A fantastic meal," I said. "Quite the best I have ever eaten."

Mr Hovanessian's face flushed with pleasure. "I'm so glad to have served you something you enjoyed", he said. "As I said before, it is unusual for us to see a foreigner. Do call again and tell your friends to look in." He and his wife saw us to our car and as I drove off I made a note of the mileage.

Of course I told many people about this meal. "Impossible!" I was told. "How could you get a meal like that in such a remote place? What traffic is there on the road, apart from lorries bringing in caviar from the Caspian Sea, and troops moving up to the Russian frontier?"

It so happened that three months later I had to make another visit to Manjil, this time with an English engineer who had been one of the biggest sceptics. The circumstances were identical. We were both tired and hungry and reached the plateau at about the same time.

"Here we go then", I said, looking at the mileage. "Just another five miles."

Sure enough, after five miles, we reached the village, unmistakably the same one because of the pile of rocks with the one balanced on top. But of the *tchae-khana* there was no sign, nor was there any evidence of such a building having ever existed. I asked one of the villagers. "*Tchae-khana*? There's never been one in all the time I've been here, and that's 40 years."

We drove disconsolately away. Naturally, my companion scoffed, but there was a hint of doubt, even fear, in his voice.

I can offer no explanation. I only know that I definitely had a meal in this village in a *tchae-khana* that I have ever since called the world's best restaurant.

Tony Clark, Alderton, Gloucestershire, 1993

UNEARTHLY ADVICE
The following event happened more than 30 years ago when I lived just outside Hay-on-Wye in Powys, Wales. I must have been 17 or 18 years old at the time. In those days, it was not uncommon to see young lads fishing off the bridge at Hay on a summer evening. One day, I arrived on the bridge by bicycle along with my fishing rod, some flies, worms and lead weights in my pocket. It wasn't the best of days. The wind was rather strong, so I weighted the line well and used some worms for bait. I was quite alone, but for the occasional car passing.

Out of the corner of my left eye, I caught sight of a man approaching down Bridge Street and onto the bridge. I was roughly in the centre of the quite long, concrete bridge. As the man approached I could see that he was a vicar or minister of some kind: grey mac, bowler hat, dog collar, white hair. He looked about 65 years old. He came up and asked if I had caught any fish and I told him I hadn't.

"Why don't you try straight down there?" he suggested. More to please him than anything else, I thought I would try the location he indicated as the current ran fast under the bridge and the water was some 40ft (12m) below. I dropped in the worm, with its heavy weight on the line, just as he started to walk back the way he came. Almost immediately, I hooked a huge chub.

I turned to call the man, but he had vanished. There was no way he could have made it across the bridge into Bridge Street in the few seconds that seemed to pass. I couldn't lift the fish up, it was too heavy, 40ft (12m) of nylon line straining to lift it out of the water. So I jerked the line and snapped it. Then I wondered if the man had leaped off the other side of the bridge, but thankfully when I went to investigate he was nowhere to be seen. I wound up my line, jumped on my bicycle and rode up Bridge Street into Broad Street, in the hope that I would find him, but he was nowhere to be seen.

There were no other witnesses to this event and no car had come along to pick him up. I went home to tell my parents. I was adamant about what happened and have puzzled over it ever since. I don't believe he was a ghost, as we had a short conversation. Was he perhaps from a parallel universe?
RB Williams, Brecon, Powys, 1997

DIVINE PROTECTORS

HELPING HANDS

On two occasions, an 'angel' or 'divine protector' has apparently come to my rescue. Around the autumn of 1984, when I was about seven, a group of friends and I went on a conker-hunting adventure in a local park. Supervising us was a responsible adult whose own son was in the party. The best horse chestnut tree was high on a steep slope and, with the adult leading the way, we climbed the slope in search of the best conkers that might have fallen in the undergrowth. We spent a while collecting a bagful and were ready to set off back home. We had been right round the park and were all a bit tired.

We took a short cut and found ourselves climbing another slope towards a bridge that hung high over the stream below. This manmade slope was relatively safe – or so I thought – and was a good 6–8ft (1.8–2.4m) wide. There was a fence to our right and a sheer drop to the left. Being the smallest, I trailed at the back while the others clambered up carefully and jumped over a fence that led to a

footpath and the streets of home beyond.

I impatiently tried to sneak past one of the others, but was nudged out of the way by a girl in the party. I slipped and lost my footing, falling to the left and the sheer drop, which was about 50–60ft (15–18m). Nobody noticed I had slipped, and everyone else managed to jump over the fence to the footpath and safety. I was left clinging to the slippery brickwork and earth, and hanging precariously over the edge where, should I let go, I would surely fall to serious injury, or even death. Time seemed to stand still. I screamed in panic, but nobody heard me. It was rocky down below and I couldn't bring myself to look. I clung on with all the strength I could summon and prayed to my maker for help.

Almost at once, I felt somebody grab my ankles and take my body weight. The physical sensation was very clear indeed. The hands moved down and formed a 'ledge' for me to stand on. But this was impossible, I thought. No one could hover 50-odd feet in the air and support my weight. Yet I felt immediately safe. I knew the 'hands' wouldn't let me fall.

A brief moment later, I heard shouts from above. The supervising adult had rushed back and was lying face down on the ledge, ready to pull me to safety. If I could reach out with my arm – which had just healed after a complicated break – he'd haul me up. I knew I didn't have the strength – or the will – to do it. Before I could build up the bottle to let go and reach up for the adult to grab me, the same 'hands' pushed me up with no effort at all – in fact, I felt curiously light as if levitating – and I was in the arms of my rescuer, who threw me over the fence to safety. I quietly thanked the 'hands' and said nothing to anyone. Whenever I walk over that bridge, which was just a few yards from where I clung on for dear life, a shiver runs down my spine.

Twenty years later, I was walking down a rolling, hilly footpath in the same park. I was listening to my Walkman, with a camera slung over my shoulder after a morning shoot. It was a bright sunny day, but the park was relatively quiet. Not wishing to waste my day off work, I'd fancied a stroll and took my camera with me. I had walked all around the park, seeing almost no one until a smiling old chap greeted me by the lake, doffing his flat cap. I said "Good morning" and went on my way.

A few minutes later, when I was walking down the hill just a few yards from the lake, I felt a hand reach out and gently push me to my left, where I clumsily rolled over, a bit dazed, and still with "Live and Let Live" by Love and Arthur Lee pounding in my ears. I looked up and saw a 'trial' type motorcycle speeding on down the hill. No vehicles are allowed in the park, except for the warden's, so I had no reason to worry about engine noise and impending danger behind me.

I wouldn't have heard it anyway because of the Walkman, and the rider wouldn't have been able to see me ahead as I had just rounded a sharp bend. In that split second when I was pushed, the bike had whistled by only inches away. When I got up, I couldn't see anybody around apart from the guy on the bike in the distance. Could the old chap who greeted me have been my 'guardian angel'? It seemed weird that there had been nobody around until a few moments before the incident, when I said good morning to a stranger.

The park where both incidents occurred is called Boggart Hole Clough, so named because, according to local folklore, a farmer and his family were driven off the land by a boggart, a mischievous sprite. If my rescuing hands were not those of a kindly dead relative or 'spirit guide', could they have been a boggart's? Since my experiences there, I've always quietly asked for protection wherever I go. I don't know who I'm asking, but I know they've helped me out before.

Paul Hughes, Moston, Manchester, 2004

CB SAVIOUR

In August 1987, I was living in St. Louis, Missouri, and I had to make a trip to Indianapolis for my divorce hearing. I left right after work on a Thursday evening and was travelling eastbound on Highway 70 through Illinois and into Indianapolis, listening to the radio and singing out loud as I do when I'm driving alone. All of a sudden a very clear 'voice' in my head said, "Turn on the CB".

I wasn't in the mood to listen to the CB so I just thought, well, that was weird and shrugged it off. Not 15 seconds later the 'voice' said, "Turn on the CB!" with an air of urgency. Again, I ignored it. A few seconds later the 'voice' screamed in my head "TURN ON THE CB!!" Not sure what was causing it or what to do, I turned the CB on. The first and only thing I heard was a man's voice saying: "We have a drunk with no headlights travelling westbound in the fast lane of eastbound Highway 70. He just passed mile marker 178."

As this was said, I looked up and saw the mile marker 177 sign. I instantly moved to the far right lane, and not more than two seconds later the drunk flew past me, heading in the wrong direction, in the lane I had just been in. I have no doubt that the warning saved my life that night.

Rhonda L Perry, by email, 2002

A BURMESE APPARITION

I served with the Gloucestershire Regiment during World War II. I left South-ampton on 10 January 1939 on the troopship Dunera, arriving in Mingaladon, Burma, about a month later. This was a military cantonment about 13 miles (21km) from Rangoon.

At about 2am one morning in December 1941, I was asleep in the corner of the barrack room. I had my mosquito net down and tucked in tight around the bed. The room contained 12 beds, six on each side. The entrance was off a verandah at the opposite end from where I lay. All the others were asleep, except for one man, who was out shooting small game.

I was sleeping on my left side when I was awoken by someone kneeling on my bed. He had dark hair and brown skin and looked very Burmese. I thought someone in the room was fooling about, so I told him sharply to move off. Then I heard my friend arrive back from his shooting trip and I asked him if he could see anything. He said no, but he told me later that he had felt a presence and his hair had stood on end with fright.

I again said in very harsh words for the figure to move off or I would hit him in the face. He just stared at me with a sort of half smile. I struck out, but my fist went into empty air. I got really scared and hit out frantically. The mosquito net broke, and through the ripples of the net as it fell I could still see the smiling oriental face. I rushed out the other side of the bed and my friend put the lights on. This woke up all the others and we searched everywhere but could not find anything. No one got any more sleep that night, and about 11:00am I went to the garrison church and told the Padre what had happened. He had no sound advice for me. I thought he might have carried out some sort of service or exorcism.

Not long afterwards, my Regiment was ordered to move out of the barracks into the jungle to face the Japanese advancing from Pegu towards Rangoon. I didn't see the barracks again until I returned to Burma in 1947 as a Military Adviser to the new Burmese Army. Mingaladon had many air raids both by the Japanese and later by the British when they reoccupied the place. The only building to receive a direct hit was the one where my barrack room had been – this room no longer existed. I was told that it had been hit the day after we moved out. I believe that the apparition was a warning for me to get out as soon as possible.

Ben Robins, Ealing, London, 1992

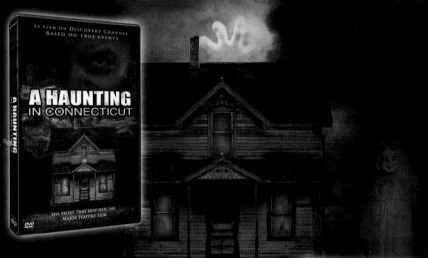

2 Creature Features

The behaviour of animals is frequently beyond our comprehension, and we often make up for this by imputing human motivations to them. Do some of our fellow species have mourning rituals? Why do certain animals muster in congregations? Could these gatherings be the equivalent of human law courts or parliaments?

The following accounts offer fertile fodder for speculation.

ANIMAL MAGIC

THE HARE AND THE CAT

On a crisp October morning in 1998, I found my beloved black cat Billie (twin sister of Bessie) lying outside near the cat-flap, cold and dead. She appeared unmarked, but upon closer inspection I discovered a small round hole in her back, as if she'd been stabbed with a biro. When I turned her body upside down, red blood poured out – her heart had been pierced. I was devastated, but also very confused; I live in an isolated rural location, there was nobody around who could have stabbed her, and it was highly unlikely that she had fallen on a nail or sharp stick. Cats tend to land on their feet.

I rang my neighbour to ask him to help bury Billie, and while waiting for him to arrive I wrapped her in a blanket and placed her body near the tree under which I have been burying my pets, which was around the other side of the house, near the kitchen door. I then did a bit of weeding to take my mind off what had happened.

After my neighbour dug a hole, we buried Billie with her favourite toy, and I sadly resumed my gardening. I turned my back on the house to dump some weeds onto a pile, and when I turned again there was a young hare crouched outside the kitchen door, staring intently at it. It hadn't been there three seconds before. I crouched down level with the hare and in my grief and confusion, asked it: "What are you doing here?" To my horror, it turned, looked me straight in the eye, and opened and closed its mouth several times, like a fish, making a little popping sound. I was totally thrown; why was a wild hare trying to speak to me? And why didn't it run away when I put my face near it?

I reached down to pick it up and move it away from the house and out of my sight. It hopped slowly away from me, around the back of the house, and came to rest in the exact spot where I found Billie's body. This time, when I reached down to pick it up, it let me. I was still wearing my rubber gardening gloves. I held it gently and began walking towards a copse of trees on the edge of my property.

Suddenly it made a little start, as if waking up from a dream, and lashed out with its back legs. The claw on its hind leg tore straight through the glove on my left hand, across my wrist. I held the hare at arm's length and said: "It was *you*! You're the one that killed the cat!" At that instant the hare stretched itself out, opened its eyes wide, and died. I shakily carried it over to the trees and laid it on the ground. It was unmarked, with no sign of injury. I inspected the claw on its hind leg; it was the exact size and shape of the injury in Billie's back.

I retreated to my kitchen to have a calming cup of herbal tea. I worked out that the cat had caught the hare, which probably went limp while it was being carried back to the house as a present for me. When Billie tried to get through the cat-flap with it, the hare objected, lashed out with its hind leg, and stabbed Billie in the back, piercing her heart.

The only way I could understand how the cat died was because the hare appeared to tell me. Is it possible that the spirit of the cat had somehow entered the hare's body at the point of death, and stayed there long enough to solve the mystery? I have read that hares were once thought to possess magic qualities. Based on this experience, I am inclined to believe it.

Susi Mulligan, Asterby, Lincolnshire, 2007

LUNAR CAT

Anyone who owns a cat will be aware of diverse gruesome ways in which they dispatch their prey; but I would be intrigued to hear if anyone else knows of a cat that drowns mice – and then only on the full moon. On four consecutive full moons, Mandrake, a one-year-old moggie, has captured and brought in a mouse, drowning it in the dog's water bowl by forcibly holding it underwater. This is not behaviour observed at any other time. So far, friends have suggested he is

> **❝ A hawk landed on the Harley's seat and remained perched there for three days ❞**

offering sacrifices to the Goddess Diana or catching and killing evil witches that have changed themselves into mice; or perhaps he catches mice on the full moon because he can see best at this time, and discovered accidentally that a mouse would drown if put in the dog's water bowl. On the last full moon (16 May 2003), no mouse was drowned, a fact perhaps explained by the total lunar eclipse. Does anyone have an explanation for Mandrake's behaviour, or has anyone else had a similar experience with their cat?

Richard Gipps, Oxford, 2003

HAWK PAYS LAST RESPECTS TO BIKER

An American friend of mine here in Thailand lost his battle with cancer at the age of 42. From his early years until his death, he had been an avid motorcyclist, his favourite machine being the Harley Davidson. A few years ago, he became one of the founder members for the Pattaya Chapter of the Harley Club, and he was still the treasurer at his death.

The club often went on treks lasting several days, but the last one my friend came on, he drove the service van because of declining health. For three days his coffin lay at the *wat* (temple) so all of his many friends could say their last good-byes. His favourite Harley Davidson was parked alongside. The logo of a hawk stood out brightly on the fuel tank.

Two hours after the bike was parked, a wild hawk landed on the seat and remained perched there for three days. Some observers said that the bird was injured and could not move or fly away, but those who knew him well saw this as a message from him. When the time came for the cremation, the hawk flapped its wings, took off, circled the *wat* three times and disappeared forever. Goodbye, old friend.

Raymond J Conduit, Pattaya, Thailand, 1996

RESPECTFUL SPARROWS

I have two bird feeders in my garden that I keep topped up with seeds and nuts. These are adjacent to a thick hedge where sparrows hide and sometimes nest. Most mornings there are 15 or more sparrows flitting from the hedge to the containers, creating an entertaining sight that my wife and I would watch from the kitchen window. My wife became ill with cancer and her last weeks were spent at home, during which time the sparrows continued to entertain her. On the morning of her death (at home), the sparrows disappeared and didn't return until after her funeral eight days later. It was as though they were paying her their respects. Very strange!

W Ford, Bramhall, Cheshire, 2006

SHEEPISH MANOEUVRES

Driving near Hereford last year, I noticed a flock of sheep, all of which (with only a few exceptions) were walking slowly in single file in two parallel lines across the slope of a hill. There were no other people or animals around, the sheep didn't appear to be walking from or to anywhere in particular, and they didn't appear to be keeping to any clearly defined tracks or paths. Unfortunately, I couldn't wait long enough to see whether they eventually did an about turn and started walking in the opposite direction. Can anyone offer any explanation?

David Cotton, Leicester, 1998

TRIAL BY FIRE AND WATER

Finding it impossible to enjoy her garden because of the large numbers of ants, my mother decided to destroy the six large nests that had appeared in her lawn. Conventional poisons had little effect, so in desperation we poured paraffin on each nest and set them alight. We thought the problem was solved.

A couple of days later, we went to check the nests and found hundreds of ants scurrying about carrying tiny white eggs they were apparently rescuing from the ruins. Fearing new nests, we boiled kettles of water and poured them over the blackened heaps. No insects could survive that treatment – or so we thought.

The next day, the doorstep, the window sills and even the roughcast of the walls were brown with what seemed to be tea leaves. A closer inspection revealed several lines of ants stretching from the back of the house to the ruined nests on the lawn. The ants were collecting the dead bodies of their fellows, carrying them about 30ft (9m) down the concrete path, and leaving them outside our house, to show us what we had done (or so it seemed). Then they went back for more, even bringing dead eggs. The work was clearly well organised.

We were so unnerved by the ants' revenge that we took no further action against them, despite the fact that within a few weeks, the nests were as busy as they had ever been.
Valerie Button, Cullompton, Devon, 1997

FALLING FRENCH FROGS

While staying in Villeneuvette, near Montpelier in the South of France, my partner and I were woken at 8.15am on 11 August by our four-year-old daughter Erif who came to show us, proudly, a small frog she had found in her bedroom which she was sharing with her seven-year-old sister, Effy. Erif also informed us that there were two similar frogs dead on the floor. We discovered that there were in fact over 20 dead frogs on the floor. The vast majority were discovered underneath the open window (the only open window) of the fourth floor bedroom. During the previous night, there had been an atypical, dramatic storm; a veritable 'horror movie' tempest. There is a lake a few kilometres away and the surrounding area has a conspicuous frog population in wetter weather.

It would seem that the frogs somehow gained access to the room via the window. There was sufficient water on the inside to indicate that a substantial amount of rain had got in. The most interesting explanation is that the storm sucked up the frogs and deposited them through the window. However, there were no frogs either outside on the terrace below or on the outer sill and the window was no more than 3ft by 4ft (90x120cm) – so if was a classical fortean frog fall, it must have been incredibly localised and well aimed. There seemed no reason to suspect that the frogs had clambered down from the roof (there was no prior example of frogs in the upper parts of the house, according to the owner); and why would they all (apart from one) be dead? The idea they somehow climbed in from the ground also seems ridiculous. Can anyone offer an explanation?
Simon Price and Effy Brooks Price, Laxfield, Suffolk, 2005

BEASTLY GATHERINGS

COW'S ELEGY

Several evenings ago, some friends and I were walking on a local hilltop and we came upon the carcass of a dead cow lying in some long grass. I would estimate that the carcass had been there for a couple of days, but due to the difficult terrain it had not been removed.

Later that same evening, immediately after sunset, all the cows and calves on the hilltop started to move urgently but silently along the fresh cowpath that led past the carcass. All the beasts, without exception – young and old – gathered in a circle around the dead animal, their heads lowered and tails motionless. After several minutes, during which time the cowpath stragglers had caught up and joined the others, they started to slowly slip away into the dusk.

A strange and somewhat eerie sight, and one that had quite an effect on all who witnessed it. Were the beasts responding to some telepathic herd instinct and saying goodnight to one of their kind – or were they ruminating on the transient nature of their existence?

Alan Price, Lisvane, Cardiff, 1979

CAT CONVENTIONS

I witnessed a strange phenomenon during the summer of 1977 or 1978 when I was helping the local Friends of the Earth group to renovate an old warehouse which is now used as their headquarters. During the course of this work, I was examining the roof of this building, which had been abandoned for several years and was in a very neglected state, when I descended into a courtyard about 20ft (6m) across, strewn with rubbish and surrounded by low, disused buildings. A gate to a narrow side street was, I think, locked, and the overall impression was that the area was no longer often disturbed by man. In the middle of this courtyard was a semicircle of six to eight typical feral cats, thin and in poor condition, sitting on their haunches and apparently looking at another cat in the middle of the semicircle, also sitting and facing them.

This latter animal was of very different appearance from the others, being well fed, with a healthy-looking if untidy coat, and very much larger. It seemed to be bigger than any domestic cat I have seen before or since, although not by a dramatic margin. All the cats seemed to be adults, and my impression was that they had been sitting absolutely motionless until disturbed. I can't recall whether they were making any noise, but in any case I only had a second or so to observe the scene as the smaller animals fled in all directions as soon as they saw or heard me. The big one, however, didn't run or even get up, but turned and looked straight at me. In view of its size and obvious lack of fear, I believed I was in some danger, and so climbed over one of the walls of the courtyard and escaped into the street. I thought this experience was strange, as cats are not social animals, but had no idea how rarely it seems to be reported.

Chris Peers, Erdington, Birmingham, 1988

Several years ago while I was living in Ohio, I was awakened by the sound of what I assumed was my neighbours' son crying. It was summer, and in my neighbourhood it was typical for us to leave our windows open to catch a breeze. Having been awakened, I decided to use the bathroom, and on the way, glanced out of our window at the neighbours' house.

It was about 2–3am, and the night was clear and bright with the light of the moon. Sitting at the top of our neighbours' back porch steps was the biggest yellow tabby cat I have ever seen. It was sitting in profile to me, and appeared to be "addressing" a group of about 10 smaller cats of various sizes, colours and markings, which were sitting in the yard in a semicircle with their attention on the tabby.

As I watched through the window, the tabby slowly moved its head back and forth, all the while making the crying sounds I had first assumed came from my neighbours' son. The motion of the cat's head was very odd – slow and robotic, side-to-side, as if continually scanning the semicircle of other cats. As I said, the other cats appeared to be listening raptly.

Deciding to get closer, I crept out the back door and quietly sat on my own porch. At one point, I cleared my throat. The big tabby turned its head slowly toward me with the same robotic motion and stared. The other cats looked at me too. After a few seconds, the cat audience quickly and quietly dispersed. The tabby continued to look at me and then seemed to return to "normal" cat behaviour. He/she washed his/her face, slowly turned and walked away. I had never seen the tabby before or since.

Do you think I saw the "King/Queen of the Cats?"

Barbara Ashton, New York, 2008

> **66** *The cat turned its head slowly toward me with a robotic motion and stared...* **99**

ANT CIRCLE

When I was a child living in Rickmansworth, Hertfordshire, I spent a lot of time during the summer holidays in our large garden, watching insects. We had a path made from a single row of paving stones that ran along the side of the bottom terrace, following the washing line. On summer afternoons, I used to lie face down on this path, watching the comings and goings of the black ants that used to build their homes between the slabs.

Once I saw a red ant that had come into the garden from one of the many huge red anthills in the wild land next door. It attacked a black ant, and there was the inevitable fight to the death. While the ants were fighting, a crowd of black ants gathered and stood in an orderly circle watching. After the red ant (as expected) had killed the black ant, the onlookers surged forward. The red ant made good his escape, without any hindrance. One of the crowd picked up the dead ant, and with the others all following slowly in single file, made its way back down the hole between the paving stones.

Mrs Sandy Gibson, By email, 2002

CROW CIRCLES AND MAGPIE COURTS

In the mid-1970s, when I was in my teens, I saw a "magpie court" in the school fields on the edge of Lewes in Sussex. Half a dozen magpies strutted round, circling a magpie on its back with two other birds holding it down by its out-stretched wings.

Although the prone bird had its beak open, it seemed not to be making any serious attempt at retaliation. I didn't observe any feathers being pulled out.

Occasionally, one of the circling birds moved in to peck the prone bird. There was no suggestion of this being a squabble over food. I suppose there was a slim possibility that the bird had simply fallen on its back – but magpies are not particularly flock-oriented, so I can't see why the other birds would be "helping" it.

I stood watching at close quarters for some minutes through the chain-link fence that bordered the school football pitch, with the birds taking no notice of me at all. I was impressed by the number of magpies gathered; this was before the population explosion of these corvids. In my earliest years it was rare to see any magpies.

Alan Gardiner, Burgess Hill, West Sussex, 1999

A few years ago, I was walking on Wiveton Downs, near Blakeney, Norfolk, in late summer. I came across a circle of nine magpies with one in the centre. The magpie in the centre appeared to be the leader, and larger than the other magpies. It seemed to be giving orders or instructions to the other magpies, perhaps juvenile birds.

Paul Brooke, Holt, Norfolk, 2002

While I was driving from Inverness to Perth (but not by the A9) during the 1970s, the road turned to the left and I could see over the wall or edge into a field. I saw a circle of crows about the size of the centre circle of a football pitch. All the crows were facing inwards and in the centre were two other crows. As the road turned to the right I lost sight of them.

Edwin Airey, Shipley, West Yorkshire, 2002

I witnessed an interesting gathering of magpies some years ago. I was driving past an area of mown grass in a university hall of residence. One large crow was surrounded by about a dozen magpies that were harassing it. One at its back would rush forward and peck the crow. The crow would turn – and the same thing happened again, but the remaining magpies were keeping a respectable distance from the crow. I watched this game from my car – so it was not obvious to the participants that a human being was nearby; perhaps had they realised this they would have flown away. This went on for a minute or two.

Suddenly, the crow pinned one of the magpies to the ground with one foot – and immediately struck it through the eye with his large beak. For a fraction of a second everything froze – and then the magpies flew off. The crow strutted up

and down for about 10 seconds and then flew away. The magpies returned and started to tug at the leg of their dead companion. Each one in turn paid the body some attention – and they tugged it several feet, before they gave up and dispersed. Elsewhere I have seen magpies taunting a cat – but not in such numbers and not in a circle on the ground.
Ken Baron, By email, 2002

While working temporarily for Cardiff City Council as a litter picker in 2001, I came to the Gabalfa playground in north Cardiff around 3pm. I was picking up rubbish when a great cloud of birds – around 150 to 200 ravens, crows, magpies, blackbirds, pigeons, sparrows – landed some 20 metres (66ft) from me and assumed a circle. In the middle, two ravens pinned down a crow and were hitting it with their beaks and claws; once in a while other birds joined in. Several times the crow tried to escape, but was brought down by the ravens. After a good 20 minutes, they all took off.
Mario Fiorillo, Cardiff, 2003

At about 11.30am on 19 April 2005, I heard a terrible 'caw-caw' noise. Assuming it was the local cat attacking a crow, I looked out of my window to see a magpie and a crow attacking another crow. The attackers were quite mercilessly pecking at the crow, which was huddled up on the ground, though the magpie seemed the most aggressive. This carried on for about five minutes. I went to another window but by then the birds had gone, though the magpie came back for some worms.

I first thought this was an (albeit small) crow court, but later realised that it didn't entirely fit the description: for one thing there was no patient, silent circle of crows around the 'offender' and while courts usually involve only one species (often crows) and there are cases of one species 'trying' a member of another (e.g. rooks trying a jackdaw, see letter in *Daily Mirror* 11 June 1975) it seems odd that a crow would ally with a magpie against a fellow crow; I had thought that birds of different species didn't flock together. This seems less like a crow court and more like some kind of inter-avian mafia, with the attack seeming more like a back-alley beating or intimidation rather than a judicial punishment.

This isn't the only odd bird behaviour I have seen in Durham. In May 2004, I saw a huge bird parliament. Durham has for a few years now had a remarkable number of very large and bold crows. One day while revising, I looked up to see at least 300 crows flying in a huge circle over my lawn. Other crows kept arriving until there was a huge ring of crows flying overhead. After about 10 minutes of circling and cawing, they seemed to have reached some kind of decision and began to fly off, in groups of two or four, in a very definite direction, as if some feathered general had given them their orders. Perhaps Durham is home to some kind of avian parliament? I had thought bird parliaments were less common these days, what with our countryside disappearing and biodiversity falling, or maybe Durham's reclamation by crows shows that birds are still very much organised.

Ian Kidd, St John's College, Durham, 2005

We first saw a crow circle about 8.00pm on a Saturday evening in the early summer of 1984 as my husband and I walked the dogs along our country lane. The fencing surrounding what was the second field away from the road had crows perched along the four sides. There were literally hundreds of birds, one perched on each post and others on the fencing between the posts all the way round the field, but I can't remember whether there were any in the centre of the field.

I returned home for my camera. The resulting photograph was poor as it was a gloomy evening, but it did show dark outlines of the birds perched on the fencing.

Looking out from our living room window, we have seen two other crow circles, both in the evening. The first time there were several circles of birds, one inside the other, but on the second there was only a single circle and therefore fewer birds. I can't remember whether there were any birds standing inside the circle.

One afternoon, from the living room window, we saw a flock of wintering sheep standing for some time in a circle. Eventually, they just moved away.

Christine Bretherton,
Brougham, Cumbria, 2002

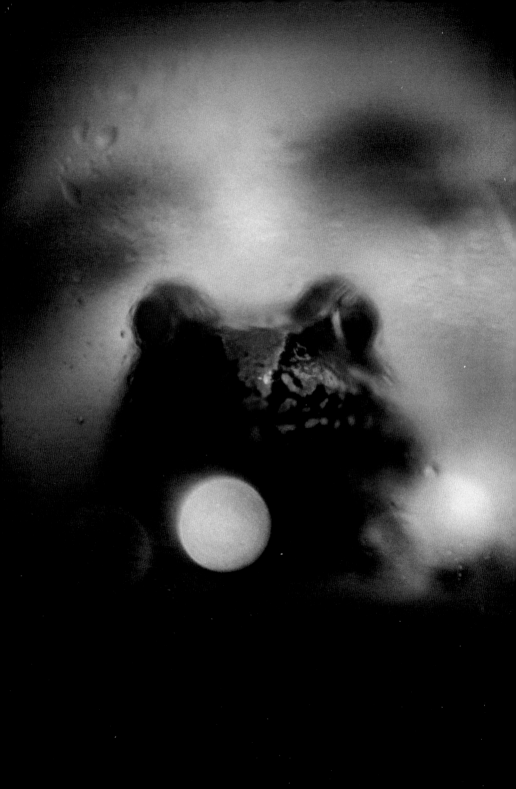

3 *Ghostly Gifts*

It seems impossible that solid objects - and sometimes even living creatures - should appear out of thin air. And yet many people have experienced the sudden and inexplicable arrival of coins, stamps and other items apparently from the void. Such phenomena, of course, offer a challenge to the laws of physics; but maybe there's a realm where these laws don't apply.

CREATURES FROM THE VOID

FROG EX NIHILO?

When I was about eight or nine years old, I enjoyed experimenting with baking soda and vinegar – which, if mixed together, foams up and produces carbon dioxide. One day, I had the bright idea of using this principle in the construction of a small bomb. I took a large glass peanut butter jar and filled it halfway with vinegar, suspended from the metal lid a quantity of baking soda enclosed in a tissue paper packet, and then tightly sealed the lid onto the jar.

My parents' home in Grand Rapids, Michigan, is situated atop a steep hill, which is overgrown with vegetation. This hill overlooks a small lake. Having constructed this sinister instrument of destruction I went out back, shook the jar vigorously to combine the two elements, and tossed it down the hill into the vegetation to avoid flying shards of glass. I waited 10 minutes for an explosion but it never went off; I left disappointed, and would have entirely forgotten the incident if it wasn't for what happened a few months later.

My father hired a college student to cut down the weeds on the hill with a scythe in order to provide a better view of the lake. After having worked on the large hill for some time, the fellow came up to the house with something in his hand and said, "Did someone put a frog in a jar and throw it down the hill?"

I was dumbfounded. He had the still tightly sealed jar in his hand – the bomb that never went off – and floating around in the swill was a large, dead, frog. He was as puzzled as me, and I'm sure he wasn't trying to pull one over on me, since he was totally unaware of my chemical experiment. Furthermore, it is essentially impossible that anyone else would have put the frog in the jar since it was hidden in the thick, steamy vegetation; the vines and plants were so tangled and profuse that nobody would climb that hill for fun. Finally, the house is not located in a travelled area.

Around this time (that summer, or the one before or after) there was a great storm. Lightning hit the well about 15ft (4.5m) from the house, which is on top of the hill I tossed the jar down. The house shook from the huge explosion and I can well remember the terror of my sister and me, who were playing! We rushed into my mother's room for comfort, and our housekeeper, who was similarly startled, came running up the stairs. She had been (perhaps fortunately!) sitting on the toilet in the downstairs bathroom, only about 30ft (9m) from the well. She was more shaken than the rest of us for, as she reported, while she was sitting there ball lightning ("a ball of fire", to use her words) came up out of the sink and floated out through the closed bathroom window!

Needless to say, I have no idea how the frog got into the jar or if there is any connection with the lightning strike, since I'm unable to date it precisely. One thinks of spontaneous generation or the modern experiments of passing electrical currents through a soup of water and gases that result in the form- ation of amino acids. The story has an alchemical ring to it: could a more sophist- icated chemical bomb create a *homunculus*?! More obviously, it resembles the toad-in-the-hole phenomenon.

David Fideler, Grand Rapids, Michigan, 1986

STONED WEEVIL

In November 1976, I had just eaten a mango and gnawed the stone clean, when, placing it on the hearth, I saw it move! The stone continued to give small jerking movements and I examined it closely. A mango stone is very hard indeed and I could find no crack or opening on the surface. I broke it open with nutcrackers and out fell a very wobbly beetle, pale pink, which I recognised as a common weevil, totally without pigmentation. It seemed very weak and cold, so I warmed it up by the fire. It became quite lively but refused to eat, and was dead the following day.

Michael Walton, Aberdeenshire, 1986

PENNIES FROM HEAVEN

When I was eight years old, living in Chicago, Illinois, I went to the corner store to buy milk. I really wanted a Milky Way bar; they were 10 cents back then, and I had no money to spare. I lugged the milk home and as I got to our apartment door, it began to hail. I liked to pick up hailstones and put them in the freezer to try and keep them. I began gathering stones. Then I saw an odd grey one. Something was inside and I melted it in my mittened hand to find I was holding an American Mercury head dime. I looked up, thanked God and went back in the hailstorm to buy my Milky Way.
David T St Albans, by email, 2000

When we lived at our previous address, three silver sixpences appeared in random places around the house over the course of a few weeks. My husband and I didn't possess any when we moved in some six years earlier and they ceased to be legal tender before we were born. The only connection we could make with the number three was that I became pregnant three times while living there, although one resulted in a miscarriage. If pressed, my sceptical husband will confess to seeing an old lady at the foot of our bed on more than one occasion. We have since moved but have kept the sixpences, for luck perhaps?
Annie McEwan, by email, 1999

One day in January 2000, upon going to her (part completed) jigsaw, my wife found a 1939 12-sided threepenny bit among the pieces. It was not there when she left the puzzle the day before, and she never pours the pieces from the box, but always carefully picks some at a time.
Michael Billing, Henstridge, Somerset, 2000

In the summer of 2000, our recently founded Tunbridge Wells Fortean Society was investigating a 'haunted' pub in that town. One of the reported 'manifestations' consisted of coins turning up in unlikely places, for instance in the middle of a newly cleaned table in the kitchen after the pub had closed. Since these were mostly little five pence pieces, I have tended to disregard them, since it must be the coin most often lost.

However, on one visit I ordered a pint, hung around while it was drawn, then joined the group. I paid with a note and received the correct change. Some time later the barman sent over a message saying that I had left something on the bar.

I thought this was unlikely, but I went over and there was a 'wooden' 12-sided threepenny bit (that's what we called them when I was a boy), dated 1938. The barman is young and professed never to have seen such a coin (which was last minted in 1967). He insisted that he had only noticed it after serving me.

Ian T Peters, Lamberhurst, Kent, 2000

On 7 December 1999, I found a coin on the linoleum floor of my kitchen in Kentish Town, north London, an hour after it had been swept. I collected coins as a boy and so recognised it as a Russian one-kopeck piece, but it was not from my collection. The worn copper coin bore the date 1800, and a large initial letter π (P in Cyrillic), standing for the mad Czar Paul (1796–1801). The only other people who had been in the kitchen that day were my wife and a friend who had come to stay and had just flown in from Virginia that morning. We considered the possibility that he had been handed the coin as small change either in the US or the UK, and then inadvertently dropped it on my floor, but rejected this as the Kopeck piece bore no resemblance at all to any current US or UK coin. So… I am obliged to accept (tentatively, of course) that it was apported from the warehouse of the Cosmic Joker.

Paul Sieveking, London, 2000

I visited the College of Psychic Science in Kensington for a group sitting with three other people in 1967. I've forgotten the name of the medium, but I do recall he was quite expensive, which was why the hour was shared by the four of us. When it was my turn for his attention, he said: "You may find this disappointing, but all I have to say to you is that if you ever think something odd is happening, look for the number 17."

The following day I was in my flat in Acton, west London, listening to a discussion on the radio with the film actor Omar Sharif talking about God. While listening, it occurred to me that if there really is a God then none of us have anything to fear. Just as that thought passed through my mind, I heard something fall in the gas meter cupboard in the kitchen. There was an old penny sitting on top of a pile of shillings I kept in reserve to feed the meter. Where had it come from and how had it managed to balance on top of a pile of shillings? Then I remembered what the medium had said. I picked up the penny and looked at

" I recognised it as a Russian one-kopeck piece, but it was not from my collection "

the date, 1934. Then the penny really dropped: adding the numbers together made 17.

Four years later, I was living in a rented cottage in Drayton, Somerset. As an actor, I have often experienced periods of prolonged unemployment. At that time, the unemployed spell had continued far longer than usual. One evening, in desperation, I said in a loud voice, "If there is anyone around, do something to give me a little encouragement! To give you some time to think, I am going to make a pot of tea."

When I returned from my small kitchen with a cup of tea, I noticed a sixpence in the centre of one of the large flagstones that made up the floor. Taking a piece of string, I measured from the coin to each corner of the flag. It was sitting exactly in the middle. It was not on the floor when I left the room and if it had fallen I would certainly have heard the noise. I picked up the sixpence and read the date, 1961. Again I realised that the sum of the numbers was 17. I still have the penny, but sadly the sixpence has disappeared.
Colin Bower, Sherwood, Nottingham, 2002

A few years back – 1994 I think – I was walking up the stairs of the house I shared with four friends in Wichita, Kansas, and noticed a US two-cent coin, dated 1864, lying on the carpet in front of the coat closet at the top landing. Everyone in the house denied ever seeing it before. The same went for friends who visited frequently, and a couple of others who had lived there before me. Our group had lived in that house for about four years, and I had been there a total of about two years (in three different stints). Since no one claimed the coin, I kept it.

I've no idea where it came from, and neither do my friends, but some of the stories I've heard them tell about that house might indicate some kind of presence: a toaster that toasted bread even though it wasn't plugged in; a phantom whistle that two of the guys heard (each thought the other whistled, and they determined that it had come from a spot somewhere *between* them); cats that would stare at or play with absolutely nothing; and heavy footsteps in the living room upstairs while everybody else was downstairs in the den watching TV.

Bart Smith, Jr, Independence, Kansas, 2000

In about 1988, when we had lived in our house for about a year, a farthing appeared on the stairs. We explained this away by deciding it must have been trapped between the skirting board and the stairs and released by vibrations. But our money-finding didn't end there. We were staying in a guesthouse in London (when attending the *Fortean Times* Unconvention) and, on unpacking our luggage, found two halfpenny pieces. The luggage was fairly new and the halfpenny had long been out of use.

Once home, we continued to find halfpennies around the house. Over a period of about four months, we found over a dozen. In the end, I thanked 'Them', but pointed out that the coins were no use as they were no longer legal tender.

Anthea Holland, Clacton-on-Sea, Essex, 2000

AS IF FROM NOWHERE...

PARANORMAL PASTRY

I did my usual rounds before retiring for the night. The doors were all locked and everything was in its place. We got up at 7.30 the next morning and while I made the bed, Jan went downstairs to make a pot of tea. No sooner had I plumped the first pillow than I heard her shouting frantically, "Quick, come and look at this!" I raced downstairs to find her pressed firmly against the back door. With mouth open wide and a shocked expression on her face, she stood pointing at the kitchen floor.

I was standing in the hallway looking in, so I had to make my way into the kitchen and past the breakfast bar to see what she was pointing at. There in the middle of the room, placed precisely at the centre of a vinyl floor tile, was a

small fruit pie. The cake box, a plastic Tupperware container about the size of a one-litre tub of ice cream, was standing on the worktop. But it was positioned underneath the shelf on which it is normally kept and where it was definitely sitting the night before. Strangest of all, when I examined the box I found that its lid was tightly sealed.

I could just imagine one of my children climbing up onto the worktop, opening the box and removing the pie before replacing the lid and jumping down again. And I could also imagine one of them sitting on the floor about to eat it. The trouble is my grownup children left home many years ago and the two of us live alone! Or do we?

David Bent, Burgess Hill, West Sussex, 2006

INSTANT STAMP COLLECTION

In about 1998, I found an unused 1995 American stamp on the floor of our lower bathroom. I don't collect stamps and I hadn't visited America and neither had my flatmate. I still have it. When I woke up on 9 February 2000 and was hauling myself from my bed, my hand rested on another stamp. This time it was from Thailand – it had been used and has half a postmark on it.

I have never been to Thailand and I do not know anybody who has been there who would send me a postcard (which the stamp may have fallen off). It had not been in my bed when I went to sleep. Oh – and a couple of months ago, I found a New Zealand coin on my bedroom cabinet. I've never been to NZ and I don't collect coins or stamps.

Judith Lunny, Norwich, Norfolk, 2000

BALI TEASPOON

For nearly a month in 1983, I stayed at Puri Saraswati Bungalows in Ubud, Bali. One night, a little after midnight, I woke to see in the absolute darkness a tiny point of pure, shining light floating above my bed, about an inch (2.5cm) across and 5ft (1.5m) above me, nearer to me than the rafters. As I watched, it occasionally moved very slowly a few inches, irregularly and in different directions. It was nowhere near the ceiling fan; there was no hole in the roof; and I had no other source of light. After several minutes, I switched on the light by my bed, and the spot disappeared.

Some days later, I was sitting on my veranda writing, when a teaspoon materialised 6ft (1.8m) up in the air and fell with a clatter to the tiled floor

" There was a toaster that toasted bread even when it wasn't plugged in... "

4ft (1.2m) away from me. It was a totally still day, and there was no joker in the bushes. It couldn't have been thrown, as it fell vertically. The veranda was 11ft (3.4m) high, but it had not come from that height; there were no rafters or cornices from which it could have fallen. I owned no teaspoon and there was no cutlery in the bungalow.

What annoys me is that there seems no hidden message in a floating white light, or in the materialisation and fall of a teaspoon. If the gods speak, they choose a damned cryptic way of doing it.

Ken Lake, Loughton, Essex, 2000

LAVATORIAL CASH MACHINE

I finished talking to my boyfriend on the phone around a quarter to one in the morning and then went into the bathroom. After I brushed my teeth, I decided to do some tidying. The bathroom has a lot of glass shelves. I started to dust them and put the toilet lid down to kneel on to reach the high ones. I dusted the top and when I looked down there was a £20 note sitting on top of the toilet seat perfectly flat as if it had just come out of a cash machine. I had my pyjamas on and my purse was in my bag in the living room, so I've no idea where it came from. When I checked my purse later on, there wasn't any money missing. I texted a photograph of the banknote to my boyfriend. He suggested I say "Thank you" for it, so I did – and at that moment there was a knock on my bedroom door, even though I was alone in the flat. I've put the £20 in a safe place and have vowed to start dusting more often!

Jennifer McGhee, Greenock, Scotland, 2005

Not every odd thing seen in the sky fits the classic 'flying saucer' description – for instance these accounts of noisy clouds, black holes, and even a flying man. And all kinds of puzzling things can be encountered closer to the ground, such as spooklights or cowled 'grim reaper' figures. Perhaps the strangest (and grossest) yarn here concerns the Alabama road strewn with nameless viscera.

MYSTERIOUS FIRES AND LIGHTS

EVENING SPARKLER

In late summer 1992, around seven in the evening, my two dogs and I were having our usual ramble along a disused railway line. It was a narrow path, with trees and shrubs bordering each side. The sun was setting, throwing spears of light between the trees. Up ahead, about 20ft (6m) away, the mutts had stopped dead in their tracks and were regarding something – an odd sight which rooted me to the spot, too. We were observing what at first seemed to be a large sparkler! It was bright orangey-yellow, circular in shape, roughly five to six inches (13–15cm) across and 'hovering' about 4ft (1.2m) from the ground. It seemed to be on fire, throwing off sparks the same way a sparkler would. A crackling noise could be heard. I must have gaped at it for around 20 seconds, then glanced down at the dogs, noting their reactions, then looked up again. It was gone!

Walking forwards, I reached the spot. The sun had long since dipped below the horizon, ruling out a trick of the light. On the ground below where the 'ball' had been hovering, I noticed scorch marks and a tiny flame on the point of going out. The twigs and leaves were blackened – physical evidence, at least, that *something* had been there.

Friends had various explanations: fireball, ball lightning, Martians, fairies, gnomes, Armageddon on a small scale. You name it, they came up with it. Come on chaps, heads together – what was it?

Mrs M Gunn, St Albans, Hertfordshire, 1994

LOUD CLOUD

The following occurred while I was observing the Hale-Bopp comet for the last time before it disappeared into the vastness of space. I think it was either at the end of April or early May 1997. I had set up my telescope in my back garden and had an excellent clear view of the comet. As I looked though the telescope, I heard a very strange and loud noise directly above my head. I can only describe it as a mixture of the whine of a jet, the throb of a propeller engine, and the sound of a large stone enclosed in the slowly rotating empty metal drum of a clothes dryer.

Looking up, I saw a very low, whitish cloud containing a number of lights, which reminded me of round car headlamps in a fog. It was not moving at any great speed and was, I estimated, about 200ft (60m) above the ground. Then I noticed the lights were uniformly spaced in the shape of a horizontal letter T. The word "Spitfire" came into my mind. Reflecting on it since, I imagined a Spitfire would have similar dimensions at that height. The surrounding cloud was not much bigger than the T.

I then noticed a second cloud to my left, which also contained lights of a similar intensity. It was travelling parallel with, and close to, the first cloud, at the same speed. The lights within this cloud made no discernable pattern. More words came into my mind: "Keep going, you can make it." In less than a minute, both clouds disappeared over nearby houses and the noise died away.

At no time did I feel alarmed, just very curious. It was definitely a UFO, but whether it was some kind of spiritual experience, a ghostly replay of a World War II event, or the effect of some unknown technology, I have no idea.

Anthony Hampton, Willenhall, West Midlands, 2005

WAS IT A TULPA?

The thing that I find most unusual about collecting fortean reports is that until you have actually experienced a fortean event, you have that nagging sense of uncertainty that these things really do occur. I can say unequivocally that they do exist, because I experienced one in 1974.

I was walking home at 4pm one day in mid-October 1974 when my attention was drawn to what looked like a giant, white-hot air balloon about 100ft (30m) off the ground. As I watched, it suddenly started to decay at the edge and turn black. My first thought was: "My God, someone has set the thing on fire!"

It gradually stabilised until it looked like a round black hole in the sky. I was only half a mile (800m) from home and literally ran the rest of the way. I burst in the back door, grabbed my 8mm movie camera and managed to get about 3ft (90cm) of film exposed before the vision vanished in the west. Later on, my mother informed me she had also seen the same object about the same time or *earlier* than I observed it, and it exhibited the same behaviour exactly. My only conclusion was that somehow the original object travelled backwards in time or else there were two identical objects exhibiting the same behaviour.

Since that appearance in 1974, I have read about the creation of thought-forms or tulpas and wonder if somehow either my mother or I inadvertently created one that was observed by the other. It was certainly a remarkable experience, and I can well appreciate the feelings of those who are reluctant to inform others of something weird that has happened to them. Despite myself, I was far from comfortable with whatever had happened and kept trying to mentally explain it away, even though I have collected and read about unusual phenomena for years. I have had several other unusual experiences but none were so definite and unequivocal as this one. Then too, I had the strip of movie film which although unspectacular shows a clear and definite black dot above the trees.

W Ritchie Benedict, Alberta, Canada, 1980

TENNESSEE SPOOKLIGHTS

I practised medicine for many years in a rural area of east Tennessee. While there, our family purchased a large farm some eight miles (13km) from our home, occupying a deep secluded cove surrounded on three sides by wild mountains. Over the previous 175 years, it had been occupied by numerous families who made a living farming, timber cutting and distilling whiskey. A large number of murders had occurred in the cove, the victims' bodies buried in a small, overgrown cemetery on the farm.

Several years after we bought the place, hunters and young couples who liked to park in what was known as the Orchard Field began to tell me about seeing a "ghost", numerous times over many months. It carried a pale green light. Sometimes it drifted through the woods, apparently on the ground, and sometimes it floated through the air from a point high on a nearby mountain. It almost always came to rest at the eastern edge of the Orchard Field, very near where the last owner of the cove lived in a small house, and where he had been murdered. If the light was disturbed by a shout (or a pistol shot), it vanished instantly. If left alone, it would remain motionless for a long time near or on the ground, then drift off into the dense woods and disappear. I took my family to the field on several dark nights, but we didn't see the light.

One night, before leaving the hospital at 11pm, I called my wife, then drove to our cabin on the farm to spend the night. The day had been warm and wet, typical for April, and the night in the cove was very dark and damp, with a faint fog. When I arrived at the cabin, I made a cup of coffee, turned off all the lights, and sat down on the dark front patio. Frogs were making music along the shores of the lake 100ft (30m) in front of the cabin, whippoorwills were adding their songs from the fields across the lake, owls were hooting on the wild mountainsides, and far back in the cove, coyotes were faintly howling.

After sitting perhaps 10 minutes, I became aware that the frogs and whippoorwills had suddenly stopped singing, and within a few seconds I caught sight from my right of a flicker of green light in the dense woods north of the partially cleared land around the cabin. It appeared to have come from inside a deep gorge, called the Thurman Hollow, after the man who was murdered there 100 years ago, some 400 yards (370m) north of the cabin.

The light, which resembled the diffuse glow produced by the carbide headlamp often used by local night hunters, rambled gently around among the trees and finally emerged in the small field south of the woods. Here it paused for a long time, as if it were looking at the cabin. After a long, silent wait – the whole hollow had become silent – the light floated gently through the field to the small road I had used to reach the cabin. Here it paused, again "watching" the cabin for about five minutes. Then it began to float evenly up the road toward the cabin and came to rest some 100ft (30m) from me. I could see nothing attached to it, and was unable to assess its height above the ground because it shed no light on anything around it.

At last it moved through the large pines downhill to the lake shore directly in front of the cabin, stopping again. I backed carefully until I touched the cabin wall, then edged my way towards the electric switches. After a long spell, it started up the slope directly toward me. When it reached a point just 20ft (6m) from the patio, I threw a switch and the area in front of the patio, clear to the lake, was flooded in bright light. I saw no movement. Nothing was there. I turned

> **I caught sight from my right of a flicker of green light in the dense woods...**

off the lights. The pale green glow had disappeared.

I never saw the light again, but a few years later two local night hunters in the Orchard Field saw a bright green light in the air high up on the mountainside. They heard screams. They quickly left, reporting the incident to the sheriff's office. It so happened that a small plane was missing, and at least 100 searchers spent the night inside the cove. The missing plane was found days later, miles away.

I'd like to say that what we all saw were one or more ghosts, but I'm not sure – there might be a more mundane explanation. In east Tennessee, we have a large number of fireflies every summer. The larvæ of these beautiful insects spend their time before metamorphosing in early summer burrowing in damp leaf beds, especially in leaf drifts in small streams. They are fairly large and full of a thick liquid. They make good fish bait. The larvæ themselves glow dimly in total darkness. When a hook is inserted by a night angler, the leaking fluid glows brightly. The angler's fingers glow for a long time. For this reason, local fishermen call the larvæ "glow worms". For fish, glow-worms are a succulent titbit, and I feel sure other land and airborne critters like them just as well.

I believe several local species of animals scratch these glow-worms up for food, especially in the late spring when the worms are largest and full of juice. And I believe whippoorwills, though they catch most of their prey in the night air, also eat these larvæ in the spring. Whippoorwills, though skilled flyers, spend a lot of time on the ground. Rooting glow-worms from leaf debris with snout or bill would result in a messy face, which, in the dark, would shine. One night in early

May, after the above incident, I saw the small, shining face of a raccoon from a distance of 200 yards (180m).

I like ghosts. I've seen more than one. I hope I'm wrong about the glow-worm theory. Seeing a ghost sounds a lot better.

Dr Rufus S Morgan, Signal Mountain, Tennessee, 2004

Julia Morgan-Scott, Dr Morgan's daughter, adds:
The Appalachian cove described was also the site of a mini-UFO flap in the late Sixties, when schoolchildren saw a UFO sitting in a field, if not the one described in my dad's story, then very close nearby. The day he saw the "ghost light" he had discovered the moonshine whiskey still of the murdered previous owner of the cove, and the pieces were sitting on the porch where he sat. I like to think that the light he saw was the old moonshiner come to fetch his copper still.

EERIE ENCOUNTERS

ROCKETMAN

The following happened one July in the late 1990s. My husband and I were lecturers at the local further education college at the time, and were attending a colleague's retirement party. The party was being held in a modern house in the village of Fremington, between Barnstaple and Bideford in north Devon, and a mile or so from the River Taw. It was a warm, still evening, so several of the guests were sitting quietly chatting in the garden.

I glanced up at one point and saw the dark shape of a figure of a man moving, upright, steadily and silently across the light, evening sky, roughly west-to-east. I looked across at my husband quizzically and he smiled and nodded, as he'd seen the man too. None of the other people in the garden took any notice of the flyer, so I began to think that this must be some kind of regular local occurrence that didn't warrant comment. After the party, I talked to my husband about what I'd seen, and he confirmed the sighting – the figure of a man, wearing a kind of rucksack, with no obvious means of propulsion – no jets, no wings, no parachute, nothing. As the figure was against a clear sky, with no landmarks, it was difficult to estimate height, but we thought he was something like 60–100ft (18–30m) up. This wasn't a sighting of a balloon or other piece of aerial debris – it was definitely a human shape moving, apparently purposefully but in a relaxed way,

across the sky.

I was amazed to have seen such a thing, and that no one at the party but the two of us had apparently noticed it. My husband said there was nothing mysterious about the sighting; it must be one of the military trying out a jet pack or some such. We had seen something like it in James Bond films, so I assumed his explanation was feasible, but always remained puzzled, as I'd never seen anything like it before – or since. I must add that both of us were completely sober when we saw the figure!

Elaine Towns, Barnstaple, Devon, 2008

MEETING THE REAPER

In 1986, I was 17 and studying engineering at Brooklands technical college in Surrey. One evening, I was walking along the path from the college to the train station. I had either left early or had been delayed. Normally, the footpath would have been heaving with students eager to get home, but I was alone. About a third of the way along the path, I decided to relieve myself against a tree. As I did so, I looked back to see if anyone was coming. It was twilight, but light enough to see. Someone was coming from over the brow of the hill, but too far to worry about, so I carried on.

I looked back again and noticed the figure had gained some 30-odd yards (27m). Thinking that it must be someone on a bike to have travelled that distance so quickly, I took one last glance before finishing and the figure had gained a lot of ground again. I walked back to the path and picked up my bag. Taking a quick glance again (thinking I should have heard a chain, tyres, that sort of thing), instead I was confronted by what can only be described as "the Grim Reaper" without the scythe.

The figure was wearing a hessian-type cloak with a black hood over the face. The cloak reached the ground and was hung over the body in a triangular-shaped fashion. I then realised that every time I had seen the figure it had been motionless as it was now, standing just 10 yards (9m) from me. It was more than 8ft (2.4m) tall. I should have been scared, but instead found myself almost drawn to it and took a step forward. We faced each other for what seemed like a few minutes but was probably only 20 seconds. When I came to my senses, I turned and jogged away without looking back. I reached a gate where I waited for the figure, thinking I might have been involved in a wind-up, but nothing happened.

Mark Sidwells, By email, 2001

> ## _"The figure was wearing a hessian cloak with a black hood over the face"_

CLOAKED IN MYSTERY

I read Mark Sidwells's account of an encounter with the "Grim Reaper" with surprise and delight, as something very similar happened to me. In the Fall of 1999, I was living in Roslindale, Massachusetts, a small Boston neighbourhood. My house bordered on the Arnold Arboretum, a large (by Boston standards) park of rolling fields and forest. Like many area residents, I spent a large amount of time in the arboretum, walking and biking. Around dusk one evening, I was walking down from atop one of the park's many hills. A paved path runs around one side of this hill. I was headed towards it, with the aim of crossing it on my way to the path to my home. The landscape in front of me was mostly field, with the occasional tree.

I was singing softly to myself as I descended, when I became aware of someone else in the vicinity. Looking up, I saw someone moving at great speed along the paved path, coming in from my left. Embarrassed to have been caught singing, I glanced down again quickly, but something struck me as strange. This figure was moving much too fast to have been walking, so I originally assumed he was on a bike (hardly unusual in a public park.) The problem, I realised, was that there was absolutely no sound, no gears shifting, no hum of tires on the pavement, nothing. And why, I thought, was someone riding a bicycle while wearing a long black cloak?

I looked up again and watched the approach. He was big (the eight foot estimate that Mark gives sounds about right) and skimmed along over the ground without any evidence of a bike. He starred fixedly ahead and since our paths were perpendicular I never saw his face clearly, just the hood covering it. I found it difficult to focus on the cloak; my eyes wouldn't stay in focus when I looked at it, but went watery and blurry (nothing else in the area produced this effect). The figure struck me as frightening in an out-of-place sort of way, but not menacing or malevolent.

I remember thinking "I must be seeing things" and closing my eyes for a second or two. When I opened them, the figure was still there, and was passing right in front of me. Then he simply vanished. This I couldn't easily swallow, so I walked around for a while, examining the landscape to see if he had dodged behind a tree or suddenly veered off course, but there was no sign of him. My first thought afterwards was that I had seen the Grim Reaper on a bike, and I laughed it off a bit, although it has baffled me ever since.
Jeff Stevens, By email, 2001

AN OFFAL EXPERIENCE

Here is a report of a very strange night in the early autumn of 1989. At about 1:30am, we were driving along a country highway between Montevallo and Alabaster in Alabama. It was overcast and there was an oppressive feeling to the air. We both became uneasy, but chalked it up to nerves. As we continued to drive, the impression that something wasn't as it should be increased, and I drove faster, eager to get out of the country stretch of the road and into a lit-up area. I was a student at the University of Montevallo at the time and I had driven that road hundreds of times, but that night it felt different.

When we got to the intersection of Highway 31 with I-59, we smelled a horrible stench and I began to lose traction on the road, which seemed wet, although it had not rained recently. Slowing to turn into the Coosa Mart, I noticed that the road was covered in offal. There was an area about 400 yards (366m) long covered in animal parts, organs and viscera (at least I hope they weren't human). They smelled bad, but not really rotten. It was a strange smell like ozone and sulphur mixed with fæces and, well, meat.

We pulled into the Coosa Mart and asked if the clerk had noticed anything. We thought maybe a truck from a meat-packing plant had crashed, but all the clerk said was he thought he had heard it raining very hard, but when he had looked out, the parking lot was dry. Soon after, a truck driver came in and also remarked on the offal in the road. We called the local police to see if someone could clean up the mess. As my friend and I had to get into Birmingham and were already running late, we left before the police showed up.

The next day I went by to ask about what had happened and there was no evidence at all that there had been anything odd. They said the clerk had quit. I mentioned it sometime later to one of the Alabaster police officers and he said he didn't know anything about it, and suggested I not go bothering anyone else about it or they might think I was crazy and "lock me up".

As I was driving back to Montevallo, I noticed what seemed to be deep holes in a pattern resembling footprints crossing a field and then crossing Highway 115. The holes in the field were surrounded by churned earth, but on the road they seemed melted into the asphalt. A road crew was already busy filling them in. Whatever it was had a stride of about 8ft (2.4m) and left "footprints" about 16in (41cm) across. For several years, the pattern of footprints in the road was visible as the patches were darker than the surrounding road. Then they repaved the entire road. I asked around school and all anyone could tell me was they had heard there had been a one-car crash there the night we saw the offal, and that the car had burned.

Mark Warner, Ooltewah, Tennessee, 2000

DEVIL'S HOOFPRINTS

I live in a small rural town near Albuquerque, New Mexico. In December 1985, while walking outside my house in the fresh snow from the night before, I happened upon some odd hoofprints. At first I took no notice; there are many horses in the area. When I looked more closely, however, I realised that they formed a nearly straight line. Vaguely remembering a similar curiosity, I ran into my room and got a book on mysteries, which included the famous 'Devil's Hoofprints' of Devon in 1855. The drawings and measurements of the prints in the book were nearly identical to those in the snow. The hoofprints went about 15ft (4.5m) in one direction, away from the property. I followed them back and found they passed within 5ft (1.5m) of my bedroom window. I found no trace of them in the surrounding area.

I showed the prints to my father, who saw the similarity. I was only 14 at the time and didn't have the presence of mind to take photographs. I don't claim that the Devil walked by my house that night, but *something* left a few dozen aligned, cloven hoofprints in the snow.

Benjamin Radford, Corrales, New Mexico, 1993

All sorts of ghosts have been recorded at different times and in different places, from stern spectres offering words of warning to silent spooks which simply shuffle about, and even in the 21st century unnerving encounters with shades and spirits continue to be reported. Poltergeists are equally common, but a lot more troublesome... as some of the stories in this chapter demonstrate.

HOMES FROM HELL

DOWN IN THE BASEMENT

On 8 June 1979, I received my medical discharge from the British Army, and went to Edinburgh, where three friends had just completed their studies at Napier College and invited me to share their flat until I could find a place of my own. As I walked down Regent Terrace, the Georgian buildings and old cobbled streets with the characteristic gas lamps perched on the black wrought iron railings almost made me forget that I was living in the 20th century.

Dougie Burton met me at number 25a, a dingy basement flat. There were bars on all the windows, rising damp on the walls and creaky floorboards. Although the sun was blazing down outside, there was a definite air of gloom in the place and I was struck by the cold atmosphere. The living room was not so badly affected as the kitchen, which was very chilly. The flat was only big enough for two with any comfort, never mind three students and a friend, but we were chums and the cramped living didn't bother us too much.

Dougie went back to college, leaving me to settle in. I made my way down the narrow, dark hallway to the kitchen. The heavy wooden door needed a bit of effort to push open, mainly due to the thick carpet that covered part of the stone floor. The chill remained – along with the feeling of another presence.

I started to fill the kettle for tea when a voice close to my right ear barked

"Yes?". I jumped out of my skin and spun round to face the intruder. There was no one there. I searched the flat, convinced that Dougie or the others were playing a practical joke. No one was around, except the cat, huddled under the sink with hackles raised and claws drawn. Fearing ridicule, I refrained from mentioning my experience to Dougie, Derek or Colin. I reasoned that perhaps the voice had carried from the flat next door.

One hot and sunny Saturday about a week later, Dougie and his fiancée Janet went out to shop, leaving me alone. When they returned, I sat with Dougie in the sitting room and told him about the voice in the kitchen. He listened pensively without laughing, and then called down the hall into the kitchen for Janet to put the kettle on. A voice answered "Yes". It was the same voice I had heard before – it certainly wasn't Janet's voice. Dougie appeared not to notice. I led him into the kitchen: there was a chilly atmosphere, but no Janet. We stood there in silence. Then the front door opened and Janet walked in. She had gone back to the local grocer after forgetting something. After this second episode, Dougie, Derek and Colin related the experiences which follow.

The lads moved into the flat in March 1979. Strange noises started to keep them awake at night. The most common sound was of a baby crying. The sound would reverberate through the entire flat, growing louder and then suddenly stopping. Sometimes, the sound of laboured breathing would appear to follow one of them around the flat, particularly in the small hours on the way to the WC. One night, I heard this breathing sound move around our bedroom while the others were asleep. Objects, including watches and rings, would vanish, reappearing in very odd places. Colin Cree placed his watch on his bedside table one morning before dressing. Reaching down, he found it had gone. He searched under the table and the bed without result. No one else was in the flat at the time. Two days later, the watch was found in the biscuit tin which was kept in the pantry.

Soon all three young men were sleeping in the same room, fearful of the unknown presence. One cold April night, a warm furry animal jumped on top of Colin's bed. He began to stroke what he thought was the cat, talking softly to it as it purred. Dougie asked him to stop talking to himself. Asked what he meant, Dougie said that *he* had the cat with *him*. Derek McClymont then said that *he* was stroking the cat. Brian McCreadie, a friend who was staying the night, then proclaimed all three to be idiots, as *he* had the cat with *him*. Dougie leapt out of bed and switched on the light. There was no cat in the room.

One July night, I felt a heavy, furry object jump onto my bed, curl up behind my head and breathe heavily down my neck. On turning to shoo away what I thought was the cat, I found nothing. I thought the place might be infested with rats, but none could be found.

The following Sunday, Colin awoke just before 5:00am, tried to turn over and found himself unable to move. He was paralysed. The bed began to vibrate very rapidly, building up to a violent peak. He was sweating and couldn't cry for help. Something heavy and furry jumped on the bed and began to crawl up and down, its hot breath stifling his nostrils. Suddenly the bed was still, the furry thing was gone and Colin stumbled out of bed in a panic. Everyone else was still asleep, and the cat was on the outside of the living room window, its teeth and claws bared. It would not enter the flat for days.

The following night we were all lying in bed discussing the events and what we could do about them, when the sound of heavy footsteps came down the hall towards the living room door. Derek had locked the door after we had retired, and placed a stout chair against it. The footsteps stopped, the door handle began to turn, and the door started to bend inwards as if something extremely strong were pushing against it. This happened three times before the footsteps retreated. We heard the kitchen door open and shut with a slam that made us jump. No one dared investigate.

Nothing happened for four weeks. As the kitchen was quite large, Derek had curtained off the dining area for use as a bedroom, and began to sleep in it regularly, in spite of the cold and damp. Near the end of July, we all attended an all-night students' party a few miles away. Derek returned to the flat in the early hours with his girlfriend. They huddled in Derek's improvised bedroom, trying to get some sleep. Suddenly Derek snapped awake, and saw the kitchen door opening. It didn't creak or rub against the carpet, but glided open silently and slowly began to close again. Derek and his girlfriend watched, scared stiff, as it opened again, and remained open. After much persuasion, Derek decided to get out of bed to close and lock it. The door instantly slammed shut with a tremendous bang. The next morning, Derek's girlfriend said she would never enter the flat again.

Two weeks later, a Saturday, Derek was awakened by the front door being opened. It was Brian McCreadie. As he walked in, Derek noticed his girlfriend, Kirstin, follow close behind. Derek sat up, drank a mouthful of the tea that Brian

" The spirit claimed to be a French trader called Jon who had died in the building "

had brought him, and noticed that Kirstin had vanished. "Where's Kirstin?" asked Derek. Brian said that she was at college for the whole day. Derek still swears he saw two people enter the room.

It was time to try and find an explanation for all this stuff. I suggested a séance: after much debate, grumbling and general argument, we agreed to give it a try.

On 25 July 1979, at l0:30am, Douglas Burton, Colin Cree, Derek McClymont, Brian McCreadie and I were gathered round the heavy wooden table in the kitchen. There was the numbered alphabet in a wide circle with a whisky glass in the centre and the Yes and No cards on either side.

"Is anybody there?" asked Derek. No answer. Brian and I had no better luck, but when Colin asked, the glass shot to Yes. As we began to ask questions in turn, only Colin would get an answer. The 'spirit' claimed to be a French trader called Jon. He died of an illness in the building and his spirit couldn't leave. We couldn't get any more information, only that he was unhappy and wanted to find peace.

I wasn't satisfied because I thought that so many sounds and 'contact' experiences must surely be caused by more than one presence. I pressed for a further séance, which was held four days later. The same people were present, along with two female students whose names escape me. We began at 11:50pm, and this time it was Dougie Burton who made contact. I have reconstructed the dialogue from my notes…

Q) Who are you? [Erratic movement of the glass. No coherent name.]

Q) Where are you from?

A) Earth

Q) When did you pass on?

A) 21st century. [Murmurs of disbelief. I asked everyone in turn to take their fingers off the glass to eliminate the possibility of a prank. But the story remained consistent, and everyone was as mystified as I was.]

Q) Which part of Earth did you come from?

A) Another time dimension

Q) How did you die?

A) Illness which was caused by the fall-out of vehicular power source.

Q) What powered your craft?

A) Inter-React Drive

Q) Why do you answer only my questions?

A) You are my ancestor

Q) How can we help you?

A) Release me from your time-zone

Q) How?

A) I do not know

Q) Do you want us to contact you again?

A) Yes.

At this point, Brian jokingly asked: "How much is the price of petrol these days?" The glass shot across the table and fell over. The séance was concluded.

Immediately, the electrical lighting failed, and we panicked. The female students were screaming, Brian and I found ourselves wrestling on the hall floor while Dougie, Colin and Derek were trapped in the kitchen, unable to open the kitchen door, which had closed by itself. Suddenly the door opened again, Dougie lit a match, and the lights came on. The flat was ice-cold, and the two girls said they would never enter the flat again.

At 2:00pm that night, I felt a strange sense of forboding. A tremendous crash came from the kitchen, followed by the sound of the kitchen table being dragged across the stone floor and objects being thrown around. The commotion lasted a good 10 minutes, then silence. The following morning, Derek admitted that he had heard the sounds too. We cautiously entered the kitchen. Nothing was out of place.

Colin packed his things and left, followed shortly after by Derek. Then Dougie moved out to share a flat with Janet, and I wasn't going to live there alone. However, my curiosity got the better of me, and I arranged to share a room with a young hotel chef at the very top of the house. For a week or two, things were quiet, except for footsteps ascending the winding staircase.

It was 2:30am on 14 August. I had returned to the house after a night with friends (in a sober condition). As I felt my way through the dark hall to the foot of the stairs, the feeling of dread returned. As I reached out to switch on the stair light, a cold furry thing grasped my wrist. I shrieked and bolted up the stairs. I peered over the bannister into the inky blackness and saw two slitted yellow eyes staring up at me. I didn't sleep a wink that night.

The following evening, I arose at 5:30pm to start a new job as a hotel night porter. I picked up my Guinness pint mug, in which I kept my razor, toothbrush, etc., and walked down the hall to the bathroom. Realising I had forgotten my towel, I put the mug beside the bath and returned to my bedroom. I was about to go back to the bathroom when I saw my mug – *back on top of the dressing table*! I distinctly remember putting it by the bath, and I certainly didn't take it back to the bedroom.

Two weeks later, I spent another sleepless day, when the cupboard door kept unlocking itself and creaking open. I had had enough, and decided to leave the following day.

Bill Gibbons, Toronto, Ontario, 1990

DOMESTIC CRISIS

I moved to England from Canada in May 1996. I had never really believed in the supernatural until moving into the top floor flat of a huge Victorian house. My husband, my five-year-old daughter and I somehow managed to live in that flat for two years. It had been vacant for several years; it seemed the landlord had trouble getting anyone to sign year-long tenancy agreements. I found this out from a nice woman living in the flat below us. She and her late husband had bought their flat 25 years earlier. She was quite relieved to have a young family above her, as the flat below had long since been converted into a dental surgery, obviously vacant during evening hours.

At first it seemed lovely, looking past the years of neglect, but it wasn't long before strange things started occurring – it was almost as if the flat was driving my family apart. For starters, in my daughter's room there was a huge black sooty streak directly above an electrical outlet. I would wash and scrub it off, only to have it return. I asked my neighbour if there had ever been a fire in the flat. She became incredibly agitated and told me that she didn't like to talk about those things. "If you keep your chin up and go about your business," she said, "everything will be fine".

It was around this time that my daughter began to develop "imaginary friends". She spoke of one in particular, a man called Robber Jones. She said that he didn't like her father because "he had a big knife". My husband did have a sword in the house, as he was practising Iaido (karate with swords). She went on to tell me that Robber Jones was killed by a big knife in France, during a big fire.

Rooms were frequently freezing, which we put down to poor insulation, but one second it would be lovely and warm, the next you would find yourself covered in goosebumps. You could literally take one step forward and feel the cold, one step back and not feel it unless you stuck your hand out. The lights would turn off and on by themselves; lights that were switched on would suddenly explode *completely* by themselves. We called in an electrician, who chuckled when we told him. He did discover that all the fixtures were actually illegal as they were pre-1940s... and duly changed them all. However, things only got worse.

I spent a lot of time alone in that flat, with my daughter at school and my husband at work. I began to experience long drawn-out periods of depression and anxiety that actually led to me hearing voices. I would hear my husband cough and go running to the door, only to find no one there; then I would hear him laughing and trying to stifle laughter, so I soon became convinced that he was playing around, and grew suspicious – we would end up fighting about the most ludicrous things. I was on the verge of a breakdown. I would be washing my hair, and then be overcome with a sensation that if I opened my eyes I would find someone ready and waiting to plunge a knife into me... I would lie frozen in the bath for what seemed an eternity before the sensation would pass. I began to see my GP quite regularly, as everything in my world seemed to be out of whack.

Pieces of my jewellery would go missing. I would accuse both daughter and husband of getting into my things, only to find the missing item back in place a day later. This would convince me that my husband was having an affair, giving my pieces to a girlfriend and then panicking and retrieving them when he realised that I had "caught him". Crazy! How he put up with it, I have no idea.

Then my husband began to have his own experiences. One morning, he laid his wallet on the bedside table only to discover it was gone when he was ready to go to work. We both searched all over and he became very agitated. At this point, I felt somewhat relieved that it wasn't just me going bonkers, and screamed out loud in the room, "Just *put* the wallet back! We don't like it here! We don't want to stay here any longer than we have to!" Both my husband and I stepped into the hallway and shut the door. We waited for a beat, and then opened the door to find the wallet sitting on the table, just where he said he had left it. We immediately left the flat. Stepping outside into the sun felt like an enormous weight was off our shoulders.

That evening, my husband decided to experiment. He took the batteries out of our remote control, and with both of us sitting on the sofa with the TV 10ft (3m) away, he yelled into the air, "If there is a ghost in here, turn off my TV. I wanna go to bed." No sooner had the words been out of his mouth than the TV snapped off. He started yelling turn it on, turn it back on, but by this point I was terrified and hysterical, begging and crying for him to shut up. Neither one of us slept a wink that night.

It was during this time that we all began to see apparitions. I guess I always assumed that ghosts would be transparent, but that wasn't the case. My husband would awake in the night, seeing our daughter standing quietly at the edge of the bed, which would wake him fully. He would ask her what was wrong, but she would just leave. He would physically get out of bed during these times and inevitably wake me to tell me that when he checked, she was asleep… and is she sleepwalking?

I would be busy with a task in the kitchen or vacuuming the landing and see my daughter happily playing in my peripheral vision. It was only when I would look at her full on and ask her something that she would stand erect and look at me with the most incredible sadness in her face. That sad look struck instant alarm, so I would go to investigate. On every one of these occasions I would find that she was actually sleeping and hadn't moved from the lounge sofa, where my husband had been watching TV for two hours – or some similar situation where she was with someone else.

None of our friends knew what was happening because we didn't want to scare our daughter or deter anyone from visits. We had a young couple stay with us for a night. I awoke at 7am to find our guests dressed and ready to go, not even willing to stay for a morning coffee! As they were close friends, I asked them what the problem was and they said, rather incredulously, "Didn't you hear what was happening?"

Half an hour after they left, they called from their mobile phone, to thank us very much but tell us that they would *never* stay in that flat again. As there were only two bedrooms, they had to sleep in the lounge. Apparently, all night long the TV and stereo turned themselves off and on. They unplugged both machines, but they continued to turn themselves on. A young woman was walking the landing, so they were afraid to leave the room. We never heard a thing and slept like babies.

We finally found a new home two months later. From the minute we walked over the new threshold I felt a warm sunny feeling, and since then we haven't had any home troubles that couldn't be explained.

In the summer of 2001, I shared a table in a busy coffeehouse with a nice couple. They told me that they had just bought a home, and finally were out of "that hideous flat". I laughed and told them that I used to live in a hideous flat, on Molyneux Park Road. It turned out to be 5C, the very flat we endured for nearly two years, and like my family, they couldn't get out of there fast enough.

Denny Casely, by email, 2002

THE NIGHT SHIFT

OKINAWA POLTERGEIST

In 1968, I was 20 years old and serving at an isolated US Coast Guard LORAN station on the island of Okinawa. LORAN is a worldwide navigation system that I believe has since been replaced by GPS. I was on late-night watch in the LORAN timer room, keeping watch over 10 or 12 LORAN timers. These were machines approximately the size of a large refrigerator, with scopes and dials on the front. They were for synchronising received and re-sent electronic pulses. The room had a row of timers down the centre, partially dividing it in half, with an electronic repair shop on the other side. There was some visibility into the repair shop area, as the machines were spaced about 18in (46cm) apart.

Several hours into the eight-hour watch, I heard a crash, and on walking into the repair area found that the metal lid from a trash can (placed under a coffee serving area) had flown off and landed approximately 20ft (6m) away. I replaced the lid and phoned the duty maintenance petty officer, who was the only other person on watch, and awake, at the time. There were only 18–20 people on the station. He immediately answered the phone in another building several hundred yards away, so I ruled him out as a practical joker.

I returned to my desk, and as I was pondering this, it happened again. I walked over, replaced the lid, and again returned to my desk (around the corner and just out of sight of the trashcan). I then heard a third loud crash. I walked around the corner of the row of timers, and again saw the lid 20–25ft (6–7.6m) away from where I had just securely placed it on the trashcan. I then heard a metallic, jangling noise. The metal stirring spoons in a water glass next to the coffee pot were standing on end and rattling around inside the glass. As I grabbed the spoons to stop them, a glass salt shaker next to the coffee urn tipped over (without my touching it), the lid unscrewed as I watched, and the salt ran out over the table top.

Shaken, I ran back toward my desk. As I approached the desk, a plastic paper tray next to the phone rose from the desk top, and flew toward me about 15ft (4.6m), then accelerated at an angle to the floor, as if thrown, scattering sheets of paper everywhere. I again called the maintenance officer on the other side of the station. By the time he arrived, the activity had stopped and never happened again, either to me or anyone else (that I am aware of) while I was there.

I remember these events vividly. Nothing like this had ever happened to me before or since. A really odd connection is that, while I was in the tiny fishing village near the station a few days later, I found out that this had occurred during the local Oban festival, also called the festival of the dead. During this festival, the dead are believed to revisit the Earth, and their souls are guided and comforted at night by the light of paper lanterns displayed near the above-ground stone crypts, as the bones of the ancestors are removed, ceremoniously washed and then returned to the crypts.
Brian Henson, California, 2003

PHANTOM PHONE CALL

Friends and I returned to a recently closed cinema where many of us had worked. Months had gone by while equipment was slowly removed, and my manager pal still had his keys. We were wandering nostalgically and eyeing anything not bolted down, but it soon grew late. Our last lap around on our way out brought us to the largest auditorium. Suddenly, the phone in the projection booth rang. Instinctively, the manager ran up the stairs to answer it. He got it

> **" I decided to call the old cinema number... and I was chilled to hear a dial tone... "**

after the third ring, but heard only deep static, and was hung up on.

When he came back down, we realised the projection booth could not get outside calls, and it was the specialised ring that could only come from another business phone in the building. However, both the office and box office phones had been swiped by employees weeks earlier. So we stood there frozen, afraid to find a killer in the lobby or a ghost in the office, before finally running out.

We made tracks for the closest home, all psyched for discussion and ghost stories. I decided to call the old cinema number – we didn't even know if it was still good. The room was quiet with anticipation and I was chilled to hear a dial-tone... scared even more that on the third ring I got answered by thick, multi-layered static – so scared I hung up.

We never returned, and the cinema sat empty for several more years until it was finally bulldozed in January 2002. I took pictures of the various stages of destruction, and the last thing to go was the solidly built projection room, sticking out of the rubble like a watchtower, complete with a projector that looked like a huge gun.

Travis Pitts, Savannah, Georgia, 2002

WATER PLANT GHOST

Like Andy Hinkinson-Hodnett [*It Happened To Me!* vol.1, p.129], I encountered a "Cut-Out Man". When I was about 25, I was hired as a labourer by the city of Dayton, Tennessee. Due to medical problems, I requested a transfer and wound up working at the water plant. This is where water is sucked in through huge pipes from the Tennessee River and treated with chemicals to make it safe for drinking. The plant was rather secluded and far away from any houses. It was lonesome on the graveyard shift, from 11:00pm till 7:00am. Nobody there but me and sometimes my little dog Rastus. But it wasn't really scary. It was spotlessly clean and well lit, and there were no cobwebs or dark corners. The only place in the plant that made me nervous was the basement. That's where the huge intake pipes from the river entered the building and the atmosphere down there was creepy – maybe menacing is a better word. A gut feeling told me to stay above ground level.

One night, I went into work at 11:00pm as usual. After saying goodnight to the guy that worked the evening shift, I started the water filters, checked all the chemicals, etc. and then settled into the chair behind the desk in the office with *One Flew Over The Cuckoo's Nest* by Ken Kesey.

I was really getting into the story and lost track of time. I looked at the clock and it was 3:00am. Then, slam! Something in the hall had fallen hard onto the tiled floor. Bang! It happened again. But there was nothing in the hall that wasn't bolted to the floor. I took a deep breath, slowly eased out of my chair and peeked through the doorless opening into the hall. To the left, I saw the closet door at the end of the hall, open slightly. Then I looked to the right, and there, about halfway to the door that led to the basement stairway, were two cabinet doors lying on the floor, the same doors I had closed and latched earlier.

I decided that they weren't hurting anyone by being there, at least until the Sun came up, so I could just stay in the office in case the phone rang or anything. I returned to my chair and wished that there were a door that I could close. And lock. But there was no door. It had been removed years earlier by Charles, an enterprising ex-employee who never let on where he hid that door after he got fired for trying to disassemble the whole building in eight hours. When questioned by the supervisor, Charles pulled a knife and began to babble about the Bible, the Great Beast, and the Book of Revelation. Charles is still in a mental institution today, 20 odd years later.

I sat back down and tried to read more, but it was impossible. I began to feel that I wasn't alone. I knew that there was someone else in the building – in the basement, to be precise, and I knew that he/it was not friendly. So I just sat there behind the desk, looking through the doorway, waiting. A terrible air of hatred and evil seemed to settle in like fog in a cemetery. I was really scared. And then the shape drifted into view. It came from the direction of the basement, floating slowly about 6in to 12in (15-30cm) above the floor. It was the

shape of a man, solid, but at the same time not solid, and it was totally black, like a human body dipped in tar. I saw the arms, the legs, the head, but no face… no eyes.

When it was exactly in the centre of the open doorway, it seemed to notice me for the first time. It turned in my direction and when we were face to face, with no more than 8ft (2.4m) of open space and one small desk between us, it very nearly scared me to death. It began to scream and reach for me, but for some reason, apparently, it couldn't cross the threshold from the hall. So it reached and reached, and the arms started to get longer, getting closer with every effort, but never quite touching me. The monster leaned inward through the door and screamed its frustration.

Now let me explain that it never made a sound that I could actually hear. It had no mouth. When I say it "screamed", I mean that it sent waves of negative energy through me. Hate and fear pulsed through my body with every lunge of that black demon. I truly thought that I was going to die from the fear. I sat there for the duration of the attack, about 30 seconds, although it seemed to be considerably longer. Finally, the thing turned its head to its left, as if it had heard something. It then glanced eyelessly back at me, turned away and floated back towards the basement.

It was several seconds before I could breathe again. When I regained my senses I was in a fœtal position in the chair, with my legs in front of me for protection. Only my bugged-out eyes were above my knees as I watched for any reappearance of the spirit. As soon as I was able to speak again, I was on the telephone, calling everybody, *any*body, just to hear a human voice. I finished my shift and didn't say anything to the day-shift guy when he got there at 7:00am. I immediately applied for a transfer and was granted it. I never went back to the water plant.

I now think I know the reason why Charles lost his mind. He thought his religion would protect him, but somehow the evil got through. And I know why the people who work there now carry handguns at all times. They're scared, but they don't know what they are scared of.

In the 20 years since this happened, I have done a little research and talked to several psychics and have learned that other people have seen these black spirits in various places and that they are indeed dangerous. So if you go out ghost-hunting (and I still do)… watch yourself. These spirits are real and they are not to be trifled with.

Jeff Revis, Dayton, Tennessee, 2005

PUSHY GHOST

During my work as an estate agent, I was once instructed to sell an unfurnished Victorian terraced house with a steep, straight staircase. The vendor warned me always to hold the handrail firmly when I was alone, as there was a 'presence' on the stairs. I made no comment, as in business the customer is always right.

While I was waiting for a prospective purchaser to view, I inspected the house to see that everything was in order. About five treads from the bottom of the stairs, I felt a distinct push in my back. I leapt down the hall, as I'd ignored the advice about the handrail.

After the house had been sold, it was surveyed for mortgage. The key was returned by a very level-headed chartered surveyor, who looked quite shaken. He related a similar experience to mine, but he had descended almost the whole flight of stairs on his back. I asked the vendor if he had any explanation, to be told that an elderly relative of his had been found dead at the foot of the stairs.

Ask any group of hardened senior estate agents and most will relate an inexplicable experience.

John F Rice, Birmingham, 2003

HAUNTED HOSTELRIES

HOLLYBUSH SPECTRE

Last winter, I decided to help out a close friend in running his pub. Set in the idyllic countryside of Derbyshire, The Hollybush in Makeney is home to a few unwelcome visitors. I had been warned beforehand of unexplained voices and figures walking around after closing. I'm a very sceptical person and passed off these notions as overactive imaginations and psychosomatic responses.

One particular morning, as I was going through the routines of cleaning and setting up the bar, I walked past the cellar door only to be roughly knocked out of the way as a man in a white T-shirt thundered down the stairs. Thinking it was only my friend in a rush, I shrugged it off and walked into the Snug. My friend was sitting in the far corner, wearing a yellow T-shirt. Automatically, I thought someone had broken in and was at this moment probably tapping off the Pedigree. We both ran down the stairs to find no one around, the Pedigree untouched and no sign of forced entry.

The rest of the morning made me feel uneasy. I began doubting what I had seen, and wondering if indeed I had become a psychosomatic case.

A couple of weeks later, I visited the pub strictly on a drinking basis. As I rounded the corner to pass the Snug, a hand shot up and grabbed my arm. I span round, heart thumping in my chest, to a small withered old lady wearing a purple headscarf.

"Sorry Love, I've got a message for you." I asked whether she had the right person, as I'd never seen her before.

"Certainly, you're the young girl I've been told about. You worked here a couple of weeks ago didn't you?" I nodded, thinking she must have been a regular I hadn't spotted.

"Well, Charlie said to let you know, it was only him running down the cellar and he didn't mean to scare you."

My stomach nearly fell out of my toes. Charlie was the old landlord who had died 20 years previously. Even stranger was the fact that the lady used to come in the pub to warn the staff of paranormal activity, and had been believed to be dead for five years. No one else has seen these two materialise, only voices and unexplained glasses flying off the shelves. When I told the story to the locals and staff, they said that the only spirits in this pub where the ones on the shelves, and I'd better keep off them.

Amy Ford, By email, 2007

WAPPING HAUNTING

In 1990, I was the landlady of a public house in London – Turners' Old Star, 141 Watts St, Wapping. The regular customers took great delight in telling us stories about a previous landlord who had hanged himself in the cellar. As this type of story is told about most pubs, I brushed it to one side and thought no more about it.

A few weeks after moving in, I was upstairs in the flat with my two-year-old daughter Leanne, who was playing quite happily on the floor with her toys. Suddenly, she started chatting in the way that small children do to their dolls and teddies. I left her playing and went to the kitchen. A little while later, Leanne started to cry, and when I asked her what was wrong, all she would say was: "It's on the wall! It's on the wall!" Had there been patterned wallpaper or pictures, I would have said it was her imagination, but the walls were painted magnolia, and we hadn't got around to putting up any pictures.

There were further incidents, and I began to think something odd was going on. My Golden Labrador puppy started to cry and act strangely. Downstairs in the bar, he was happy, calm and well-behaved; but upstairs in the flat, either on his own or with company, he would bark at the wall. One day, he started to chew a hole in that particular wall. Nothing I did would stop him – when I tied him up, he escaped, and when I shut him in another room, he barked and howled constantly. The only way to calm him down was to let him into the bar.

One night, I woke up feeling cold. Something was standing at the foot of the bed. It didn't speak or move at first, and I thought it must be a shadow. I asked who it was; it turned, went to the wall and disappeared. Soon after, Leanne awoke screaming that it was in her room. This became a regular occurrence, and then, even when the pub was open, doors held open by a hook or bolt would suddenly slam shut. Trophies and shields flew off their shelf and pictures dropped off the wall.

The pub was named after the famous landscape artist, JMW Turner (1775–1851). It is said that he would bring his mistress there. Could the phenomena have something to do with him? Or with the landlord who hanged himself in the cellar?

Mrs PE Laver, Cambridgeshire, 1996

> Some ghosts are heard and not seen; others manifest as fragrances, often indicating the presence of deceased loved ones, bringing comfort to their kinsfolk. The soundtracks of some traumatic past events can come back to haunt us too; some seem to be endlessly repeated, like the echoes of battles fought long ago, or somehow etched into the environment.

STRANGE SOUNDS

FOREST VOICE

I have lived on the same dead-end street surrounded by forest in the quiet rural village of Dorchester, Ontario, for 22 years of my life. One breezy summer night in 2001, when I was 14, I went outside to play basketball. It was around 8pm and the sun had already set. My dad walked past me with our golden retriever. "Going down to the road," he said, and left me in the driveway with only the sound of the chain mesh rattling after each basket I scored. I glanced back at the dark road and saw my dad walking out of sight.

After a few minutes, I heard three digital beeping sounds coming from the woods across the road. Thinking nothing of it, I shot a few more baskets. "Beep, Beep, Beep." It happened again. I thought it must be someone's cell phone or pager they had dropped in the woods, so I walked to the edge of my driveway to determine the direction of the sound. Then a voice called to me from the forest. "Tim! Come here for a second, I found something."

I thought it was my dad and assumed he had found whatever had made the beeping noise.

"What is it?" I shouted back.

"Just come here, hurry up, I found something. Follow my voice."

I heard a few more beeps. Then, remembering I had seen my dad walk down the road instead of into the woods, I suddenly felt terribly uncomfortable and suspicious.

"Why don't you come here?" I asked.

After a long eerie pause, the voice said, "Tim, come here, I found something."

I knew my dad didn't have a cell phone and didn't carry a pager while walking the dog. "Tim come into the woods, I've got to show you something," the voice kept coaxing me. I asked why he couldn't just tell me what he'd found and I kept getting the same responses. At this point, I realised that the voice was only using a certain number of words and phrases – almost as if it were automated and only knew how to speak those particular words.

I stepped closer to the forest and peered into the trees, but could see nothing, while the voice kept saying the same things over and over. I began to ignore it and backed away. Finally the voice stopped and I heard the digital beeping three more times. Then silence. I could see my dad walk up the road and heard the jingle of my dog's collar. He walked right past me. I ran up to him.

"Well, what did you find?" I asked.

"What?"

"Weren't you calling me, saying you found something?"

"No."

He walked into the house. I turned back to face the black forest that was now eerily silent. All I could wonder was: what would have happened to me if I had followed the voice into the forest? Would I have been seen again? For the first time in my life, I was actually terrified. From that point on, I had a disturbing feeling that something supernatural was after me.

Tim Marczenko , Dorchester, Ontario, 2009

STONE TAPE

In the mid-1960s, I was a keen member of an amateur dramatic club based in the Saint Bride's Institute in Bride Lane. This is just off Fleet Street near Ludgate Circus, close to St Paul's Cathedral. Our rehearsals were normally held three nights a week, between 7.00pm and 10.00pm. This utilitarian institute is built on the site of the old Bridewell Prison, a 'gift' to the City of London from the young King Edward VI in 1553. Initially a workhouse for 'unruly apprentices and vagrants', it later housed the insane and subsequently became a 'correctional house' for women and children. After its destruction in the Great Fire of London of September 1666, it was rebuilt with 'improved amenities' so that the public

" It is built on the site of the old Bridewell Prison and once housed the insane... "

could "spectate punishments and good whippings". It was demolished in 1863.

Always short of funds for our productions, our lively little St Bride's Players regularly held jumble sales and so, when not wanted for rehearsals in the main hall of the institute, one or more of us would often descend into the institute's deep cellars to sort the goods gathered and stored there.

On an unusually airless evening around 9.00pm on 2 or 3 September 1966, not being needed for rehearsals for half an hour, I went down alone into the gloomy cellar to price the 'jumble'. As I recall, this room measured about 20x20ft (6x6m), but it's impossible to be exact as there was no window and the meagre light from the one grimy low-watt bulb never penetrated the dark corners. Even the light through the door from the lit stairs spilled in no more than a few feet.

I had been there pricing in complete silence for about 10 minutes, when the most terrifying cacophony erupted all around me; shouts, yells – all incomprehensible – plus the noise of obviously metal objects clashing or being struck, metal against metal – in volume and ferocity the racket was indescribable. Fearful as I was, I still looked around for a normal cause. Water pipes? – the noise was all too human. Radiators? – unlikely, for even in a deep cellar at 9.00pm, it was an unusually warm evening.

I suppose the uproar lasted no more than 20 seconds but, not usually timid, I turned tail and fled back up the stairs, taking them three at a time and probably most inelegantly in my mini-skirt and high heels! Back in the rehearsal room, a fellow 'am dram' commented that I looked pale but, too confused to explain, I responded feebly that there had been "a nasty noise" in the cellar. Rehearsals continued and the subject was dropped, even though I have never forgotten my abject terror in that dungeon-like room.

A possible explanation came to me after reading Peter Ackroyd's book *London: a Biography*. Ackroyd relates that the Great Fire started on Sunday, 1 September in Pudding Lane and by Monday "had spread down Ludgate into Fleet Street", the molten lead from the roof of St Paul's Cathedral running through the streets and "glowing with fiery redness as no horse or man was able to tread on them". Even by the following Thursday, 5 September, the diarist John Evelyn clambered over the smoking ruins on ground so hot he could hardly walk, reporting that "the iron gates and bars of the prisons had all melted" in the heat and the "subterranean cellars, wells and dungeons" still belched forth "dark clouds of smoke". The destruction was only equalled by the blitz of 29 December 1940.

I now tend to believe that what I experienced that stifling evening in 1966 may have been an *aural* manifestation of the sheer terror infecting the Bridewell prison's largely female population as the inferno raced towards them on an identically hot evening precisely 300 years earlier. Locked up behind bars, what else could the poor souls do but shout, scream, shriek and bang anything – a cup, a plate, a spoon – that might make enough noise to bring salvation from that fast-approaching roaring monster?

Ackroyd relates that the official records of the Great Fire claim that only six people were killed so, perhaps, the inmates of the Bridewell, nearby Newgate and other City prisons were indeed saved by their captors. Nonetheless, it seems to me to be extremely unlikely, bearing in mind the initial apathy about the fire, then its increasing speed and intensity, triggering general panic and the gaolers' own need to retreat to safety. Also, as such prisoners were usually poor, unknown and probably despised by law-abiding folk, their deaths might well have been thought of no account to include in the official records.

In 1972, Nigel Kneale wrote a TV play called *The Stone Tape*, in which far-distant events of an extreme nature literally imprinted themselves into stones – rather like recordings on modern tape – and which could be triggered into 'replay' by certain key repeated elements – date, weather, strong emotions and so on. Of course that was just fiction, but my experience in the cellar of St Bride's Institute does make me think that he might well have been on to something.

Maggie Southam Ferrari, Easebourne, West Sussex, 2001

BLACKWALL HORROR

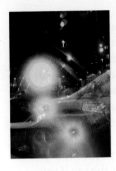

In the early 1960s, my wife and I, newly married, were living with her father in Greenwich until our new house in Kent was ready. His house, long since demolished, was in Blackwall Lane, which leads directly south from the Blackwall Tunnel. The traffic was very heavy night and day, with only a brief respite for an hour or two in the small hours until the lorries started heading north to the London docks and markets around 4am.

One dark and wet evening, when all three of us were sitting in the front living room, we were startled and then alarmed by the horrible screeching of tyres and brakes quickly followed by the scrape of metal on tarmac, succeeded by a bang which clearly meant that there had been a road accident right outside the house.

My father-in-law rushed out and across the road to try and give assistance to the motorcyclist who had evidently failed to take the sharp bend in the road, struck the kerb and then been flung from his bike, wrapping his body round a road traffic sign on the pavement. He must have been killed instantly. To this day I can still hear his blood running down the gutter.

We were all very shaken at the time, but my wife was expecting our first child and we were waiting for our house to be built, so we didn't dwell on it. Our bedroom was in the front of the house overlooking the busy main road outside. About a week after the accident, my wife and I were both woken up at about 2am by *an identical sequence of sounds*. We both said, virtually simultaneously, to each other: "Oh God, not again!" I leapt out of bed and ran to the window, which was partly open, and stared out to see – nothing. The road, unusually, was completely empty with not a vehicle in sight.

We were both so convinced of what we had heard that we assumed the accident must have happened a little further off than we had thought. I rushed out of the house. Although I went up and down the road and indeed right round the block, I found nothing and saw no one. Next day, my father-in-law, who slept at the back of the house, said that he had heard nothing; neither had our neighbours.

We made a point of reading the local papers for weeks afterwards, but never saw a report of any incident, let alone accident, which could have explained what we heard, or thought we heard.

Roy Dent, Harrow, London, 1994

SEA DRAMA

In 1985, there was a girl at the junior school in Flixton, near Manchester, which I attended as an 11-year-old, who had an interest in strange and paranormal occurrences. She claimed the house she lived in was haunted, and she would casually mention the activities of her live-in phantom – a young girl in white robes with long blond hair. She told me that once she was woken by the sound of running water and found the apparition floating above the bath next to the flowing taps. They had a short conversation, though I don't know what about.

One summer afternoon, she brought into school a pretty conch shell, white and about 5in (12cm) long. I asked if you could hear the sea if you held it up to your ear, and she told me it was better than that and asked if I wanted to listen.

It was lunchtime and the playground was full, but there were four of us huddled close together as I lifted the shell to my ear.

I heard the sound of crashing waves, followed by other noises, like the creaking and groaning of a ship's rigging. I told this to my best friend who stood next to me. He pressed his ear to the shell and said he could hear it too. Then there were drums, faint at first, but growing steadily louder, then chanting (similar to a tribal chant, but somehow more menacing).

All these sounds were crystal clear and well defined. Muffled voices and scuffling sounds were followed by a piercing scream, so loud that people 10ft (3m) away turned to look. I whipped the shell from my ear and turned to look at my friends. I didn't need to ask if they had heard it; their faces were ashen.

The girl said that the shell always did this, the noises sometimes lasting from several seconds to several minutes, but always very clear. Our experience had lasted over half a minute. She told us that from what she had heard over several 'listenings', she had the idea that the story was of a crew shipwrecked on an island inhabited by cannibals, and the fate of the sailors was rather gruesome and gastronomic.

We spent the rest of the lunchtime telling each other that we had not heard anything out of the ordinary, that it was just our imaginations, and for a time this made us feel better. But really, we knew it was not a normal event and it was definitely not a normal shell.

Jake Willott, Urmston, Manchester, 1999

ODD ODOURS

SCENTING BIGFOOT

I lived in Humboldt County (northern California) for three years, during which I was a volunteer member of the Sheriff's Posse, participating in more than 20 searches, two of which took place in the heart of Bigfoot country, the area surrounding Bluff Creek. The first of these was in June of 1988; we were attempting to locate the remains of a mother-daughter team whose disabled car was abandoned on Onion Mountain. The only trace of the daughter was a stained child's sweater; parts of the mother were found in a bears' den the following fall by hunters. The word on the Rez (the Hupa reservation, the largest in California and adjacent to the search area, although the specific search area is part of the Karuk homeland) was that mother and daughter had been taken to be brides of Bigfoot.

The second was a year later; the local Adult Retarded (this was in the pre-politically correct days) Center had taken a vanload of clients to experience wilderness near the fish hatchery on Bluff Creek. One client, in his late teens, but thinking at a six-year-old level, had a tantrum and decided to walk home, and after the caregivers drove up and down the dirt road looking for him for several hours, the Posse was dispatched to search. We arrived about 10pm, a clear, warmish night for the area, and set up the Command Post (a converted ambulance) at the Point Last Seen. The trackers headed down the road in the direction taken by the young man, and I and the resident deputy for Orleans went in the opposite direction, up Bluff Creek and away from the hatchery and any other signs of civilisation.

The deputy was called back to the command post, and I opted to walk back along the road, as children and the childlike often hide from male rescuers (most caregivers are female). I walked up the centre of the road, the mountain rising steeply to my left, the bank leading down to the creek on my right, calling the young man's name, and then heard a rustle in the dense brush on the left. The rustling was accompanied by the foulest stench imaginable, not a skunk spray, but more like an Earth-worshipping old hippie (of which there are quite a few in Humboldt, but not near the Rez) with a heavy dose of Ape Island at a badly run zoo thrown in. I stopped and asked whatever was if it was lost...

The stench got stronger and I started to panic (something I rarely indulge in); I, moved by Heaven knows what, sang "Onward Christian Soldiers" at

> ## " *It smelled like an old hippie with a dose of Ape Island at a badly run zoo thrown in...* "

full volume and off-key, and kept walking up the road to the command post. The rustling and stench stayed for about one chorus, and faded away. (Incidentally, "Onward Christian Soldiers" also repels skunks, feral dogs and panhandlers). When I reached the CP, the resident deputy asked why I was singing; I was saved from confessing my panic by word that our missing person was found (hiding in the bushes near the junction with the highway – our tracker Edith Hokman had followed his trail uphill, in the dark, from tracks blurred by vehicle tires – a masterly job).

Now some thoughts on Bigfoot: the two sightings mentioned in the article in *Fortean Times* 234, pp18–19 are approximately 35–40 miles (56–64km) apart as the crow flies, and you would have to fly, or be a really good hiker, as between the two is the Siskiyou wilderness. And in the same area, slightly to the south, is Bluff Creek. It could have been the same Bigfoot, as both areas have been burned repeatedly in the near past – most recent was the Biscuit Fire in 2002, which covered 500,000 acres (200,000 ha) and burned from 12 July to 31 December. It was put out by snow.

How has Bigfoot been supporting himself? Lots of barbecued forest animals? Has he and his adapted to eating charred vegetation? Or are the frequent reports of vandalism and theft that are attributed to meth heads and transients really evidence of Bigfoot's efforts to survive? The two sightings were on or near major arteries (major for the area). Was BF harvesting road kill? Just a thought.

Rachel Hazard, Cosmopolis, Washington, 2008

ODOURS OF SANCTITY

In May 2000, while walking down London Road towards the Elephant & Castle in south London at around 1pm, I was suddenly aware that I could smell church incense. This was not just a slight sensation; I could actually taste the 'texture' of the smell in my mouth as though I were actually breathing in the smoke. Looking around, there was nothing to indicate where the smell was coming from – no clouds of smoke or any haze in the air. There is a Catholic girls' school about 200 yards from the spot, so I thought perhaps they were having a lunch-time Mass (though I'm told that Mass would normally be over by then) and a gust of wind had brought the scent to me.

However, at around 7pm that day, as I waited for a train at Waterloo station, the smell struck me again, but this time the sensation of the smoke was so strong, I coughed. I moved slightly to see if a cloud of beatification was following me, and the sensation passed just as quickly. Again, there was no obvious reason for the smell – no maverick thurible-waving priests on platform four or sudden outbreaks of religious fervour by the Sock Shop. Nor is there a church anywhere remotely close to where I was standing.

Jonathan Ratty, Kingston-upon-Thames, Surrey, 2000

AFTERSHAVE FROM THE GRAVE

My 88-year-old grandfather died in May 2000, exactly a month after his birthday. A few days later, my mother was typing out the hymns to be sung at his funeral – hymns that had been his favourites. She was using her decrepit PC with Microsoft Word 95, and was in the middle of 'How Great Thou Art' when something odd happened.

On typing the lyrics "And when He comes with shout of exclamation, / What joy shall fill my heart", the room grew very cold and filled with the smell of my grandfather's aftershave; my mother became aware of his presence, as if he were standing behind her. The aforementioned lyrics suddenly turned bold and appeared with a bullet-point.

Now, anyone who has used Word 95 will know that it is impossible for bullet-points to appear on the screen without being formatted, unless you have already used bullets elsewhere in the document, which my mother had not. Although she is a ridiculously fast touch-typist – and very accurate too, which would rule out her accidentally pressing the control key – she doesn't have the faintest idea how to set up bullets. My mother tried to use backspace and delete to remove the bullet and bold, but without success.

I cannot explain this rationally at all; the only apparent explanation is that my grandfather was leaving a message, telling us that he was happy. It certainly gave my mother comfort. My grandfather was very religious and had been a lay preacher. One of his aunts was a medium; I have heard that this ability can run in families. My mother, my younger brother and myself have all seen, heard, felt and smelt ghosts.

H Leigh, Birmingham, 2000

PHANTOM SMELLS

The small group of paranormal researchers to which I belong recently staked out Dover Castle for an all-night vigil. Shortly after 11pm, I descended a brightly lit, stone spiral staircase from the second floor of the huge keep and walked into a veritable cloud of cloying female perfume. This was only present for about one turn of the spiral and I walked back into to it on the way up again. The limits were quite distinct. The staircase was bare of anything that could have produced such a smell — no deodorisers, for example. I checked both female members of the group, but neither had so far ascended to the level affected and there was no similarity between their scent and the one I had encountered. We experienced the same smell in a similar location on the staircase diagonally opposite at about 3.20am the next morning.

One young woman who works in Dover Castle recounted her personal experience of a ghostly smell. On more that one occasion, while standing on the ground floor of the keep, she has been enveloped by a cloud of body odour, as if a very smelly man was standing right behind her. Of course, there was no one near her. Others have experienced a strong smell of horses on the same floor, although there is apparently no record of horses ever having been stabled in the keep.

I also investigated, although in a very minor way, a haunting in a local council house. The residents regularly found objects misplaced around the house, video switches turned off etc.; but the most common manifestation was a characteristic smell, most often on the stairs. So distinctive was the smell, that it became popularly known as the Case of the Farting Ghost. A psychic/sensitive who investigated came up with the name of a deceased gentleman who, research indicated, had retired, after a personal tragedy, to the old cottages which had been demolished to make way for the existing council house.

Ian T Peters, Lamberhurst, Kent, 1996

> The term 'pixilation' has been usefully extended to cover the phenomenon of objects disappearing and reappearing inexplicably, possibly through the activity of 'pixies'. Many people have followed the time-honoured advice to ask the fairy folk or 'Good People' (politely, of course) for the return of missing objects (keys in particular), often with surprising success!

LOST PROPERTY

THROWN BY A KILN

About a year ago, the place where I work bought a kiln in order to fire-transfer patterns onto ceramic tiles. We cleared a space to site the kiln and made a small anteroom with storage space and room to work. Since then, things have been 'mislaid'. Nobody thought anything of it until we happened to mention a few incidents that together added up to 'something'.

Primarily, the problem seems to be with items 'disappearing' and then reappearing in a place that had been searched only moments beforehand. This is a regular occurrence, all with items stored or kept in the kiln room – equipment used to apply the transfers, orders for customers, stock items of tiles and so on.

This is coupled with the fact that Lesley Miller, who works in the room most of the time, doesn't like the 'atmosphere' at all. According to her mother, she is a 'sensitive', but doesn't know it. Her grandmother was 'sensitive' apparently. She postulated that the goings-on were due to her father, who died four years ago. He set the business up with his wife. Personally I think that it's something to do with the kiln itself. It was a refurbished one, and all the trouble started when we acquired it, and happens in its vicinity.

I can think of four possibilities: a poltergeist (whatever that is); some sort of time displacement, so things are there really, but people can't see them; someone playing a joke (this doesn't hold up as it would take too much organisation and someone would have been found out by now); or, finally, we are all going mad!

Claire Blamey, Great Yarmouth, 1994

THE LITTLE PEOPLE

It was with no little astonishment that I read the letter from Claire Blamey. My family and I are frequently the victim of such displacements, only ours vary slightly. As well as items being in places already checked, other objects vanish from one room only to appear in another weeks, months, or – in one case – years later. Nothing of value or importance ever goes walkabout. One of the strangest disappearances was when a horse brass that I had acquired simply vanished from a nail on the wall. At the time I was the only person in the house so I knew it couldn't be a prank. Time passed and I forgot about the horse brass until one day, being flat broke, I was hunting down the backs of various chairs for loose change. There was the horse brass, in a chair that I regularly used. Not only was the chair in a different room from where the brass had disappeared, but also it had recently been checked for another item – which I had dropped myself – and I had not even owned the chair at the time of the horse brass's vanishing. It might sound a little childish, but my family have taken to asking the 'Little People' for lost items to be returned, and by and large they are, within a few minutes.

While I was writing this letter, the phone rang. I slid the pen into the spiral binding of the notepad and made sure it was clipped in. Pens are a favoured target of the Little People. When I returned, the pen had gone. I lifted the pad up and checked the entire desktop to no avail. I asked the Little People to return the pen. I left the room and returned after a few minutes. The pen lay on top of the pad. I am currently the only person in the house.

Martyn J Renton, Yorkshire, 1994

ASK OUT LOUD

In July 1996, I was looking everywhere for my small pocket-sized survival kit that I hadn't seen since the previous February. My wife was upstairs and I had a sudden thought. I stood at the bottom of the stairs and shouted: "Can I have my survival kit back please? I don't mind where it turns up, as long as I get it back within the next few days."

My wife said she didn't have it. I told her I wasn't speaking to her and that I was "asking the spirits" for it. It sounds crazy I know, but later that day I needed to go into our attic to get something, where I was "drawn" to look in a box full of pieces of wood. To my surprise the survival kit was in the box.

I told my wife that all I needed was to find the first aid kit, which we also hadn't seen for a while, and she suggested that I "ask" for it. So I did the same thing. Minutes later, I went to the boot of my car to get something else and found the first aid kit right in the middle of the boot (it is usually kept on a shelf in our living room).

My wife thought that I was mad until she brought a woman's magazine and read a questions and advice page. There was a letter from someone who had a problem with things that kept disappearing. The answer suggested that she "ask out loud" for the items to be returned, as a malevolent spirit was probably responsible, and that being firm with them and pleasing them was a good way of getting them to return objects.

I have since done this a number of times for other items, all with complete success. Even one of my work colleagues was persuaded to try it after spending two days looking for a lost item. He was speechless when he found the missing item by his feet approximately 30 seconds after asking for it out loud.

Perhaps this happens more regularly than is reported. How often does someone put something down only to find it missing moments later – then turning up after a while in a place that you already looked? Try asking for it back; it works.
Steve Leggett, Littlehampton, West Sussex, 1998

A BOGGART'S TALE
While on holiday at a remote croft on a Scottish island in the summer of 1999, I amused myself by writing and illustrating a short story about a character called 'Maologan the Boggart'. 'Boggart' is the Scottish word for a Bogle, a mythological creature who devotes his life to creating mischief and causing mild havoc to humans by making things go wrong. He creeps about at night causing electrical appliances to malfunction and machinery to break down, and, in particular, making items disappear (and reappear when the mood takes him). He causes animals to stray and poultry to stop laying, loosens boats from their moorings and puts green slimy stuff in the drinking water. In fact, a whole catalogue of mischief. Any unexpected incidents of this kind which we humans experience are generally the result of 'being bogled'.

Since this creature is rarely seen, I imagined the Boggart to be small, with skin resembling the lichen-covered rocks. Having spent an entire day trying unsuccessfully to illustrate Maologan, I was unhappy with the result, so decided to put away my drawing and painting materials and continue the next day. On holiday, I keep all these materials in a large flightcase that has compartments for different items. Later that evening, I had an idea of how I could adapt and improve my drawing, so I opened the case to get an eraser. I had two large erasers with me, but I couldn't find either of them, though I'd used them earlier that day. I emptied and re-packed the case three times, taking out each item individually and searching absolutely everywhere, but the erasers were nowhere to be found.

Next day, I asked a friend who was going to the village shop to buy an eraser for me. When he returned with it, I opened the case to put it inside and I was amazed to find the missing erasers sitting in full view in their allotted compartment. I had been well and truly bogled!

Later that day, I told this story to another woman who was on holiday at the same croft and related some of the incidents in the story I was writing. We had a good laugh at Maologan's expense, discussing his obvious enjoyment in annoying the holiday visitors, his year-round obsession with bogling the crofters, his uncle who had moved to Hollywood and changed his name to Humphrey, and his liking for more than a few wee drams.

A short time after this conversation, she took off her wedding ring and put it on the table, forgetting about it until later in the evening. When she went to find the ring, it had disappeared and a massive hunt ensued. By bedtime it was still missing. However, on waking the next day, she found it lying on top of a book beside her bed in her tent. We couldn't explain its reappearance in the tent, as it had been 'lost' in a caravan nearby.

Several other inexplicable occurrences took place during the holiday and we were particularly incident-prone after I wrote the story. Could it be that we were so immersed in creating this mischievous character that we began to attribute minor extraordinary incidents to 'bogling'? Or had we tapped into an actual mischievous spirit who may have taken exception to my interpretation of him and my poking fun at him through jokes in the story? Who knows? But Maologan the Boggart lives on in spirit and will still be creating mischief long after the summer visitors are gone, enjoying a wee dram in his cave after a long night's bogling.

Mazda Munn, Innellan, Argyll, 1999

" *A Boggart devotes his life to making mischief and causing havoc to humans* **"**

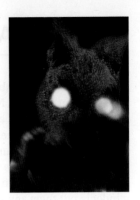

PESKY BOGGARTS

I am currently in the middle of a reasonably major, spouse-initiated, modernisation of my home. In January 2000, it was the turn of the upstairs bathroom. Various jobs were planned, but all that actually happened was the replacement of the toilet seat and flushing handle. To fit the handle, it was reduced to its five component parts.

After its re-assembly, I was of course left with the traditional single piece in the palm of my hand with no idea where it fitted. Instead of doing the sensible thing – stripping everything back down and trying again – I remember throwing it in the dustbin with the rest of the packaging.

Last month, we did a similar job in the downstairs bathroom. This time, the handle required no disassembly and I realised where the missing piece should have gone. After reading the letters on mysterious borrowings on Sunday afternoon (2 April 2000), I stood up to make a cup of tea and kicked the small, chrome spacer – the one I had thrown away 10 weeks earlier – across the floor.

So, not only do these Boggarts read minds (I had never asked for the item's return out loud), but they also seemingly scour landfills instantaneously to replace much-needed items. I still haven't got around to fitting it yet – maybe I should before it gets taken back out of spite.

Rob Grimes, Alvaston, Derby, 2000

KEYS, PLEASE!

SPOOK KEY

A year or so ago, my husband and I were living in a four-storey Victorian terraced house in Jesmond, Newcastle-upon- Tyne. One day, my husband came
home for lunch as usual and put his keys on the hall table before going into
the living room. When he left for work, he could not find his keys and, fearful
of being late, he left it until that evening to have a really good look for them.

We couldn't find them that evening, nor over the next few days. He didn't
leave the ground floor in his lunch hour, which meant that if he had absent-
mindedly put them anywhere other than the hall table, we would have found
them; the ground floor had only the living room, kitchen and hall. We looked
absolutely everywhere we could think of – even in the fridge!

A few days later, I was alone in the house when the phone rang. I went into
the living room to answer it and there, in the middle of the floor, were the
keys. The floor is wooden, so if they had been kicked or dropped by one of us
or if the cats had got hold of them, we would have been aware of it.

Helen Humphrey, Cosforth, Newcastle-upon-Tyne, 1998

HERE'S THE KEYS

In 1989, my wife and I were doing up an old house in Dumfries. I had been
piddling about with an old lock for a number of days trying to get it to work,
with little success. It was an original room door lock that would have been
fitted when the house was built. I put the lock and the set of heavy old keys
down to do something else, and on my return found the lock but not the keys.
My wife and I looked for ages but couldn't find them.

A little later, we sat down on the only two chairs in the house to eat our
lunch. Out of nowhere, the keys were thrown across the floorboards, skidding
to a halt a few feet from us! We have never tried to explain this: there was
nobody else in the house at the time.

Incidentally, a couple of years later I was going down the stairs, in the
same house, when there was a sound like a door being opened on a windy
night. Then I felt that something brushed over my head! Funnily enough
though, we never felt afraid or unhappy in the house.

Graham Oxley, by email, 2000

66 *I was absolutely convinced there was someone or something on the landing* **99**

BOGGART ETTIQUETE

In November 1999, I was standing around in my kitchen with two friends when we decided to go out into the back garden. I went to open the back door and found that the key, which we never move from the inside lock, was missing. With some irritation, I decided that my one-year-old son (who was asleep at the time) must have made off with it. With the two guests I began a fairly thorough search of the house with no result. We eventually returned to the back door and began discussing further places to search when there was a sudden noise of a key dropping. We looked to the middle of the kitchen floor to find the back door key lying there. There are no surfaces nearby, and the only thing above the space where it fell was a bare 11ft (3.3m) ceiling. All of us were at least 3ft (1m) from the spot.
Kate Brett, Semaphore, South Australia, 2000

ALWAYS WORTH ASKING

Staying in the Tudor part of the Georgian House Hotel in Haslemere in the summer of 2004, we came back to our room mid-afternoon to give our one-year-old daughter a sleep. My wife let us in as she had the room key – normally I keep hold of the keys wherever we are as she has an unenviable record of losing them. I took the two older children swimming, came back later and we all got ready to go out – I asked for the room key, and my wife immediately went on the defensive, saying that she had no idea where it was.

So we looked, couldn't find it, notified the front desk that we were keyless and went out. We came back quite late, put the children into their beds and turned the room upside down looking for the key. At the third time of looking I decided to ask for the key back, so went and stood by the door of the room and did just that. We all carried on looking, and after a few minutes my wife went to the door of the room and yelped – a large cupboard by the door had shifted away from the wall and the key was in the depression in the carpet where the cupboard foot had been.

She was quite spooked, as she'd looked under the wardrobe not long before, and we hadn't noticed either that it had moved out from the wall. Certainly, earlier on in the day it had been flat against the wall. My wife was moved to confess that the reason she'd been defensive about the keys was that she'd thought that she might've left them outside the room in a little cubbyhole by the door, and didn't want to admit it.

There was nothing for it but to say thank you very graciously and go to bed. My wife passed a very restless night – though I was unworried, as I felt that if there was anything there it was benign. I woke up at 4:30am to see her standing by my bed looking at my alarm clock, which hadn't gone off, though it was set for 4:30. She had no explanation for why she had got up and gone to look at it. I got up to go, and she told me that I couldn't leave her on her own. Ah, I said, but you aren't alone…

We checked out two days later – I nearly forgot my jacket, went back for it and for some reason was absolutely convinced that there was someone or something waiting on the landing – more than one thing, actually. Just waiting. So maybe I have now felt something.

When I told my mother we'd been staying there, she immediately said: "Oh yes, that's haunted". My eldest daughter has to be restrained now from asking 'The Poltergeist' whenever anything doesn't come to hand!
Andrew Shilcock, by email, 2004

KEY RETURNED
During the 1990s, my friend and I had a shop in Shanklin on the Isle of Wight. It was a hippie shop, and we also sold clothes. There were two makeshift fitting rooms, constructed of MDF, with a curtain and open top. Inside one of these cubicles was an understairs cupboard with a small door with the key in the lock. Its only contents were the vacuum cleaner and an ironing board. One day I walked into the cubicle to find the key had gone and the door was locked, and thought, naturally enough, that it had been stolen by some holidaymaker as a joke. Throughout the week, we were unable to open the cupboard, and by Saturday I

decided that I would force the lock with a screwdriver, as we needed to get to the vacuum cleaner.

For several minutes I twisted the screwdriver in and around the lock hoping to open it, but it was tightly secured. So I stood back and contemplated my next move. After about a minute of standing still, I felt something drop down from above me. It touched my hair as it fell vertically past me, and I looked down to see the key on the floor. As I said, there was no top to the cubicle and this key seemed to appear out of thin air. A portal of some sort maybe?

Phoenix Rhiannon, Ryde, Isle of Wight, 2005

THEM AGAIN

Regarding the sporadic letters in *FT* concerning asking *Them* to return missing items: I assumed that this was complete bobbins until I tried recently. My sister had spent the best part of a weekend hunting for some lost keys ("But I left them right *here!*"), and eventually I suggested (acting seriously, but as much out of desperation as anything else) asking *Them* to return the keys. We both addressed the empty room and said in unison, "We don't care where they are, we'd like them back, please." And then we sat down and purposefully thought no more about it.

Ten to 15 minutes later, there were the keys – a big bunch, mind – sitting on top of a pile of papers that both of us had rifled through while searching. It was my sister who saw them first, and (after going through the time-honoured ritual of blaming me) she told me how it had happened.

She'd glanced at the pile of papers (no keys there, as previously) then seconds later looked again and only *then* "double took" (I was watching her when it happened and her face was a picture). Somewhere in between the two glances, the keys had "unvanished".

A few observations: firstly, the "event" would seem to have been silent and instantaneous (and was she *made* to look again?) Secondly, shortly before the keys disappeared, my sister had quarrelled with both me and our mother – had she inadvertently annoyed something else too ? My mother, I hasten to add, isn't that puckish, and was out at the time anyway.

It wasn't scary in the least. In fact, the whole experience was almost aesthetically satisfying in some indefinable way. In fact, come to think of it, given my sister's temperament, I hope *they* take *her* next time, instead. Perhaps I shouldn't tempt the Genius Loci, though. Watch this space.

Garrick Alder, London, 2000

PROFESSIONAL OPINIONS

THE HEAVENLY PROPS DEPARTMENT

I worked for many years in a television library, where we regularly experienced the return of missing items. Our name for *Them* was 'The Heavenly Props Department'. If someone went to the vault for a tape or film and it wasn't where it should be, the rule was "the Props Department have forgotten it, give them a few minutes". The missing object was often back in its place when we looked again, no one having entered the card-access vault in the meantime. Sometimes it took longer than others – that would be "the Props Department's having a busy day". One time, the supposedly missing tape was teetering on the edge of its shelf, begging to be found. I know from talking to friends and colleagues that this is a recognised syndrome in libraries.

PJ Heaton, Horsforth, Leeds, 2000

THE PORCH TRICK

I teach in a Yeshiva in the Old City of Jerusalem. We teach college-age boys who come to study the Talmud for a year or two. The entire school has about 200 students, who are all studying the same Talmudic tracts from books that all look the same. Since people study in various rooms and until very late at night, it is common for books to be misplaced, interchanged or otherwise lost. This leads to hours of searching for the misplaced volume, opening up people's books to see if they are yours, etc.

Having read many accounts of people asking for lost items from pixies and poltergeists in *Fortean Times*, I devised my own version of this, which has become known as "The Porch Trick". The student who has lost his book goes to the porch of the school, which overlooks the Western Wall, and says aloud: "Master of the Universe, I want to study but I can't find my book. Please help me get my book back." Then the book miraculously appears in some obvious place.

This has worked without fail for all the students who have tried it (around 20 so far). They generally find their book on a table or shelf that they checked repeatedly just before. I tell them that they must search thoroughly before using this trick, and they can only use it for their Talmud, not for iPods and other objects that go missing, so as not to abuse whatever forces are at work here.

Sometimes the trick works in a more unusual way, as in this story from my student, Joel Pottesman. "I lost my Talmud for like a week, maybe longer, so I went to the porch and did the thing you told me to do. I was at lunch and Duvi Kestenbaum comes and sits opposite me and he says, 'What book were you using today, because yours was in my spot this morning?' That is how I knew the trick works." I understand that this method works in a way similar to the one described by Patrick Harpur (*Fortean Times* 209, pp54–55): that you are supposed to acknowledge the hidden forces at work, "to introduce us to the in-between world." I never had occasion to use the trick myself, but one of the other staff members used it successfully when he misplaced his own book.
Zvi Ron, Neve Daniel, Israel, 2006

PIXIE PROCEDURES

I am a 36-year-old married pawnbroker, quite down-to-earth. In our business, we have a wide selection of jewellery, and we do weekly category checks for stock control purposes. In some of the larger categories, we need to locate and ident-ify up to several hundred items. There are always five or six that prove elusive. Other staff members join the search, which usually locates the remaining items save for one or two. You can only check the same shelves, drawers, and cabinets so many times before you give up, go mad, or – as I do – ask the fairies politely to replace the item.

At first, I did this as a fortean jest, not expecting a result; but how many times does this approach have to work before the evidence leads to an admittedly unlikely acceptance of the phenomenon? I have found that certain procedures need to be followed when seeking help. The request has to be spoken clearly in a tone recognising the playfulness with which the items were removed. I have found the guilty parties to be unfailingly compliant. Typically, an item of jewell-ery three people have been looking for over several days turns up in a place we had all checked previously.
Richard Tomkinson, by fax, 2007

8 *Phantom Animals*

The spooky Black Dog of folklore, known as Old Shuck, Moddey Dhoo, Skriker, Padfoot and many other names, was variously regarded as an omen of death or a canine guardian angel, and is still encountered today – as are a whole variety of paranormal pooches, creepy cats and domestic pets which seem to be able to bilocate (appear in two places at once).

HOUNDS OF HELL

MEETING BLACK SHUCK

In 1996, my 19-year-old daughter worked for a holiday site in Hemby, Norfolk. Her late shift ended at 10.45pm, and my wife and I used to meet her after work so that we could all walk back to our caravan in nearby Newport.

One night, we delayed our return with a visit to a café and some arcades. By the time we started back along the unlit lane to the caravan, it was approaching midnight. We heard a strange noise and movements coming from the bushes to our left, followed by a snarl unlike anything we had ever heard. As we approached a house, we could just make out, behind a fence in the light shining down the garden, a dark shape the size of a large dog.

As we approached, we saw that it *was* a large dog. It stood there snarling, but unlike any dog we had ever heard – and we have always kept dogs. To say we were nervous would be an understatement. To cap it all, it had glowing red eyes. There was no way it could have been a trick of the light, as the house lights were behind it. It stood there as we walked fearfully past. After a few yards, I looked back, as the snarling had stopped. The creature was nowhere to be seen, though we had heard no sound of it moving.

Back at the caravan, my wife picked up a magazine and came upon an article

about a phantom dog that had been seen around Norfolk. The description of its red eyes and the sound it made tallied with our experience. The article said it was an omen of bad luck; since that night we have had nothing but bad luck. We still go along that lane, but we have never seen or heard the animal again.
Mr GE Thompson, Leicester, 2000

At 2:14am on 11 May 1991, I was driving home from seeing a boyfriend. I wasn't particularly tired at the time, having been asleep until an hour previously. I took the usual route home out of Worksop (Nottinghamshire) on the Blyth Road just as I had done thousands of times before. I continued beyond the streetlights and into the countryside.

I'd travelled about a mile (1.6km), almost up to Hodsock Priory when I saw in my headlights two red dots in the distance about 150 yards (137m) in front of me. I slowed right down to a crawl as I saw a huge black dog. It looked like something from hell! It had very shiny fur and a short coat; the nearest thing I've seen to it in size was a Great Dane, but it had a good 18in (46cm) over a dog of that breed.

Its ears were erect and it appeared to be dragging something quite large across the road. I've lived with dogs all of my life but have never seen anything like this creature. While I was waiting for the dog to get out of my path, headlights approached from the road ahead. The car slowed right down and as it pulled up I could see that it was a red Montego estate.

The male driver stopped and wound down his window, and I did as well. He asked me if there was anything wrong and I asked him if he could see the dog in front of my Fiat Panda. At this moment he shouted "Oh, Jesus!" and sped off into the night. I looked in front of me again, and to my joy and amazement the creature had vanished. I drove home as fast as I could. I did a little research later and found a tumulus nearby, a river and an old boundary, as well as the priory.
Victoria Rice-Heaps, Worksop, Nottinghamshire, 2000

I work on a farm in Surrey, where I live in a trailer. One night, I was investigating a strange noise just to the left of the trailer door when I had a strange sensation of being rooted to the spot; then the air seemed to get colder and I started to shake. Something moved in a nearby clump of trees, then a bat or something flew down from a tree right in front of my face. I found I was no longer rooted to the spot and went straight back in to my trailer. An hour later when I was just

"It took the form of a large black dog with red eyes that seemed to glow… "

settling down in bed, there was a bang on the side of the trailer, followed by a louder bang on the other side. I leapt out of bed, seized my shotgun and ran to the door. After what seemed like hours, something banged on the door side of the trailer and I caught a glimpse of the "thing". It took the form of a giant black dog with red eyes that seemed to glow. I kicked the door open and blasted away, but only hit the upper thigh area of its hind leg. The creature limped away at a speed much faster than that of a normal dog, and I never saw it again. All this started at around 1am and I don't know what time it finished because I went straight to bed and fell asleep.

Alex Solari, Sutton, Surrey, 2004

During 1971–2, when I was a young lad, I used to visit my friend Bob Coombes, who lived in a large, three-storey house in Claremont Road, Bristol. On numerous occasions, very odd happenings took place in the house – objects disappearing and reappearing, paint pots being knocked over. Bob's parents used to joke about a "friendly ghost", but we children were more than spooked.

The one occasion that really does stick in my mind was one evening during the summer, when we were all seated around the dining table for supper. Suddenly, the door opened and in came a large black Labrador. Seeing us, it raised its hackles and appeared scared. Within seconds, it ran for the door of the adjoining kitchen. All five of us rushed into the kitchen, expecting to corner the apparently stray dog (the family did not own a dog). To our amazement, there was no dog in the kitchen; nor was there any way that it could have hidden itself nor made an exit. We searched the house and found nothing, yet all of us agreed that we had seen a large black dog.

I gathered from my friend (with whom I corresponded until about 1974) that there were many other unexplained "strange events" and "noises" after that time; eventually the family moved away and we lost touch.

Mark Spurlock, Frome, Somerset, 1998

For a family holiday last year, I booked an 18th-century converted barn in Suffolk within the grounds of the owner's home, just 50 yards (46m) away. On the first night, I was awakened by the loudest, most intense noise – which I can only describe as crackling, pulsating electricity. Struggling to open my eyes, I stared into the face of a huge black dog. It lay on the bed between my husband and me, and as I looked down the king-size bed I realised its hind was almost reaching the end. The quilt was very heavy, as if the weight of the enormous dog was pulling it down and I couldn't move or make a sound.

Although it was staring directly at me, I felt no fear. What *did* bother me was the noise, which was incredibly loud and seemed not only to be coming from all around but also from within me. I worried that if any of our three young children (asleep across the corridor) were crying I wouldn't hear them.

I slept well again after this, but I leapt out of bed first thing to check the door was locked and the windows were all secure. Nothing could have got in. I told my husband about my 'dream' and he laughed it off. The next day, we saw the owners walking their two dogs. One of them was a black Labrador of normal size and didn't acknowledge us (obviously being used to visitors), and by the end of our week I am relieved to say I had no further visits.

Stella Maria Goddard, Leighton Buzzard, Bedfordshire, 2000

SUMMONED BY A JAWBONE?

I grew up on a farm, and around the age of 10 or 11 I was an avid collector of animal bones. By the autumn of 1982 I had rat, sheep and bird skulls and a fox's jawbone. Then I found the jawbone of a dog near our house.

One night soon after this discovery, I woke to the noise of something running around the outside of the house; it sounded like a large dog. I was filled with both fear and curiosity, but it wasn't until the next morning that I realised I had heard the footfalls throughout the beast's circuit of the building when even the steps of an adult weren't usually audible at the opposite end of the house to my bedroom. At breakfast, I told my parents, but they dismissed it as a dream.

The sounds returned a few night later, and this time it turned out my sister heard them as well. We insisted that they were not a dream, but my parents claimed that they must have been caused by a dog on the loose, though our dog was chained up at its kennel every night. That autumn, I heard the sounds a few more times and my sister heard them on at least one other occasion. Neither of us dared to peer between our drawn curtains to see what was outside. Then, a little after the new school year had started, the sounds ceased and were all but forgotten.

Whatever it was, it definitely had four legs; although there were numerous foxes and badgers in the area, I assumed it was a dog mainly from an intuition linking the sounds with the jawbone I had found. I felt that the ghost of the dog it had once been part of had been disturbed by my taking it into the house. I didn't share this theory at the time, as I knew it wouldn't be taken seriously.

The sounds of running returned in the early autumn of the following year. I and my sister both heard them on the first night of their return. When the subject was broached at breakfast, our parents lacked any explanation and resorted to "eat your breakfast" to end the conversation. A few nights later, all four members of the family awoke to hear the running around the house. In the morning, my father checked the mud path along one side of the house for footprints; he found none, though there had been no rain to wash them away during the night.

I now put forward the ghost theory I'd arrived at the year before, but no one commented as the rest of the family remained perplexed and somewhat disturbed by the events. I decided to throw out the jawbone and did so straight after breakfast. The sounds of running never recurred.

Edwin Page, Ely, Cambridgeshire, 2000

BILOCATING ANIMALS

DOUBLE DOG

In September 1998, I lost my old cross-collie dog after almost 14 years. I replaced her with a newer model – a sort of collie-black Labrador pup rescued from the local animal welfare centre. As soon as the new dog came into the house, I was aware that she could "see things" that we humans could not. At first, it became clear that under no circumstances would she venture into the corner of the room where the old dog used to sleep. She would stand and stare into that corner as if transfixed, then turn on canine heels and bolt for the back door or the sanctuary of her basket in the kitchen.

Some weeks later, we noticed that she was standing at the top of the garden, teeth bared and hackles raised, as she stared at the precise spot where we had buried the old dog. We didn't think there was anything particularly strange about this behaviour, assuming that most of it could be attributed to the dog's acute sense of smell. But we did joke that perhaps the dog was some kind of reincarnation. Probably.

Soon after this, I noticed something decidedly more bizarre going on. The small black dog began to duplicate itself. I know... perhaps I'm going mad! One morning as I sipped a cup of tea and watched the dog as she chewed a bone in front of the fire, the same dog walked right past me and through into the kitchen. Naturally, I was just a tad unnerved by this and set about investigating: no second dog could be found in the kitchen. Since then, this has happened at least twice more, with the dog "duplicating" itself and appearing in two different parts of the house at the same time. I have begun to wonder if this little black dog of mine could be some throwback to the old Black Shuck legends so well documented down the years, and that this weird bilocation is some primæval manifestation thereof... or something like that.

It gets even weirder. Last week while feeding the dog, I turned to my wife – who was standing to my right – and commented that we hadn't seen much of this canine bilocation for some time. But my wife wasn't standing to my right any more. She had been upstairs all the time and I had been talking to... well, that's anybody's guess. So far, she has only managed to achieve this feat once; but once is enough, believe me! Perhaps I *am* mad after all. I wonder if other readers have experienced anything even remotely similar. And no... I hadn't been drinking!
Paul Graham, by email, 1999

PHANTOM PUSSY

Paul Graham's bilocating dog recalls a similar experience of mine. I went to stay in a villa in Spain with my girlfriend. She took one bedroom and I took the other. After a few days, she became spooked by her bedroom and asked to swap rooms, which I agreed to. My new bedroom was unnaturally cold. I slept with two pullovers on in southern Spain in April!

Every day, a half-wild stray cat would come to our patio to beg for scraps. It

was extremely nervous and would start and look around fearfully at any noise, or if called. It would not be enticed into the house, even with titbits. Towards the end of the holiday, I was reading in the sitting room when, to my amazement, the cat came boldly into the villa from the patio and walked straight past me. I called out to it, but it ignored me and just kept going, finally disappearing into the kitchen. I immediately followed it, but it had vanished. There was no way out of the kitchen and nowhere for it to hide. I spent half an hour verifying this fact, finally accepting that I had seen a phantom cat.

That night, as I drifted off to sleep, I was awakened by a loud high-pitched scream very close by my left ear. I will never forget the sound of that scream, or its eidetic, highly distinctive, tone as long as I live. In 50 years, this is the only time I have ever experienced an auditory hypnagogic hallucination. I had not taken alcohol, drugs or medication at that time. I attribute the phantom cat, the scream and the unnatural coldness of the room to a spirit inhabiting the villa.

There are two interesting points here. Firstly, the double was associated with other contingent paranormal phenomena. Secondly, the double behaved very differently from the original cat. It boldly walked where the original cat feared to go. The double was oblivious to my call, unlike the original cat, which would start fearfully at the slightest noise. The behavioural difference between double and original has not to my knowledge been remarked in the literature concerning doubles. The next day, the original cat returned to the patio as nervous and as unwilling to enter the villa as before.

A number of questions arise here. If it had been raining, would the double have left pawprints? Would a second onlooker have seen it too? If I had snapped it with a camera, would it have shown up on the film? If I had grabbed it, would it have: proved substantial and tangible; disappeared; proved intangible; or somehow prevented me from touching it?

I have had two other "double" experiences, but with humans. On one occasion, I met by chance in a remote part of the county someone I hadn't seen for five years. He insisted that he had just seen me 10 minutes previously in a place where I definitely hadn't been. He was absolutely adamant that he couldn't have been mistaken and was cross and puzzled by my denials.

In the other incident, a builder I knew well was due to visit my house to appraise building work. On my way home, I saw him on a bus, five minutes from my house. There was no mistaking him. He was wearing the same clothes and the same distinctive hat. The only difference was that he was staring straight

" He kept telling the nurse about a 'little dog' he could see at the foot of my bed... "

ahead with a strange vacant, glassy expression in his eyes, as if in a daydream. Later I mentioned seeing him on the bus. But in fact he had come in his van!
Robert Evans, London, 1999

OUT-OF-BODY DOGGY

In 1994, I was admitted to Wycombe General Hospital in Buckinghamshire for observation, as I was worried that a heart attack I'd had the previous year was going to recur (thankfully, it didn't). In a bed diagonally opposite me was an old man in his eighties who was obviously suffering from dementia, as he said a lot of very strange and bizarre things. One morning, on waking up, he kept telling the nurses about a 'little dog' he could see at the foot of my bed. He said it was a shame to see it left there all on its own. He was so convinced that there was a dog there that, after his breakfast, he left some milk in his cornflakes bowl and asked the nurse to give it to the little dog at the foot of my bed. Everyone on the ward, the nurses included, put this down to his dementia and thought no more about it.

Later that day, when my wife came to visit, I asked how our dog, Charlie, was. She said she was worried about him because that morning she had woken to find him lying flat on his back at the bottom of the bed, stiff as a board with eyes glazed and apparently not breathing. She massaged his chest for a few minutes and thankfully he 'snapped out of it' and began breathing again.

We subsequently discovered he is epileptic and this was most likely his first fit (he was only a year old at the time). He is now on medication which seems to have put a stop to the fits. It was 8.00am when my wife found him there and it was about 7.30am that the old man asked the nurse to give his milk to the little dog by my bed. My own personal belief is that animals, particularly the more intelligent ones, are just as prone to out-of-body experiences as some human beings and that during his fit, Charlie had such an experience which was witnessed by an old man who, perhaps because of his mental state at the time, was able to perceive the dog's astral body.

Graeme Cammack, Edinburgh, 1999

CAT HERE, CAT THERE

The letters about bilocating pets struck a chord with me, as I myself had a very similar experience when I was about 18, which would have made it 1986. I had some visitors. During the course of the conversation, some new article of clothing was mentioned and I was asked to go and fetch it. As I went into the hall to go upstairs, I saw our tabby cat sitting by the front door, waiting to be let out. I opened the door and let him go. It was just starting to get dusky, but it wasn't dark enough just yet to have the lights on.

I went upstairs and entered my bedroom, heading straight for the large wardrobe at the foot of my bed. In the full-length mirror on the middle door, I could see the bed reflected clearly, with a tabby cat stretched full-length across the pillow. Completely forgetting that I had just let the cat out, I said: "Oh, Tiger! You know you're not allowed to lie there." As I said it, I realised that it couldn't possibly be my cat, although it looked exactly like him. In the moment the realisation hit, the cat appeared to become startled and jumped into a crouching position, before glaring angrily at me and then slinking off the bed, onto the floor. At this point, it disappeared out of sight and I naturally rushed to the landing, expecting to see a cat making its way downstairs. There was no cat to be seen. As for the real Tiger, no one had let him in, and when I checked, he was sitting happily in the garden. No one else had seen the mystery felid. For years I have wondered about it. I always assumed it was a spirit being, though I could never grasp why it looked exactly like my own pet.

It was not the only instance of seeing phantom cats. My mother and I both frequently thought we saw cats sitting on the stairs or rushing past our feet as we walked along. On more than one night I felt the weight of a cat land on my bed, only to discover nothing there. Perhaps the strangest thing of all is that none of these incidents have caused alarm; in fact, quite the opposite – there is something very reassuring in their presence.

Susan Topping, Newtownabbey, Co Antrim, 1999

CREEPY CATS

FLAT CATS

I find myself becoming more intrigued by the phenomenon of animal ghosts since I encountered one myself.

When my wife Jackie and I were moving into our current home, I saw a black cat watching us from the main hallway. What was unusual (apart from the cat being in our house when there was no means of entry) was the way it seemed apart from its surroundings. The effect was similar to what would be achieved if you cut a picture of a cat out and stuck it over a picture of our hall, taking no regard of lighting and shadows. I watched the cat for a moment, and then it was gone, though I cannot recall it actually vanishing.

My wife and I own cats, and one of the first jobs I had to do in our new home was to install a cat flap in the back door. The previous owners had not owned cats, so I was a little surprised to find the hole for a cat flap had already been cut in the door and then boarded over. I was slightly more surprised to find clumps of old black fur caught around the edges. Since then, both Jackie and I have seen our 'house guest' frequently, though I seem to see him with more clarity and regularity. His presence doesn't appear to bother our living cats, but may go some way to explaining why they have taken to wandering the house and yowling oddly, something they never used to do.
Chris Halliday, Coventry, West Midlands, 1999

Chris Halliday's encounter with something he believes to be a feline ghost is almost identical to an experience I had myself some 10 years ago. He describes the thing that he saw as looking as if "you cut a picture of a cat out and stuck it over a picture of our hall, taking no regard of lighting and shadows". I would have described the mysterious black cat that I saw as looking distinctly two-dimensional and sharply triangular. Another arresting feature that I remember noticing were the thing's eyes – cut-out, or almond-shaped, holes through which I could see the scene directly behind the creature (in this case, coincidentally enough, also a hallway wall) and I wonder if Mr Halliday might recall a similar detail. Furthermore, he mentions that he cannot really remember the creature vanishing, and I had the same impression. I remember the strange kind of out-of-body/timeless dissociation that I had with my immediate surroundings at the time of my viewing. The other two people with me just seemed suddenly to fade away into peripheral non-importance the instant I locked eyes with the thing.

Interestingly, this encounter also took place at about the time that I had either just gotten, or was planning to get, my first cat. Some years later, I had an encounter with a ghostly *white* cat while stepping out of the shower at my university residence; and other people living with me at the time also claimed to have seen it. Unlike Mr Halliday, though, I only saw the black cat once, whereas my own cat used constantly to see, and stare at, things that were invisible to me – could it have been this mysterious "black cat" that he was somehow sensing? I don't know.

Trevor Ouellette, North Bay, Ontario, 2000

ELUSIVE WHITE CAT
In the spring of 1995 I was, in all probability, depressed. My mother had passed away a few months before and I was "between relationships". However, I shared a house with supportive friends, and Job Seekers money seemed to last quite well.

One afternoon, I was with friends chatting in the large living room on the first floor. I was sitting on a dining-style chair when I saw from the corner of my eye what was clearly a white cat – medium-long hair, I'd say adult-sized – walk behind my legs and under the chair. It never emerged the other side – in fact, I never saw it again. Thinking back, what amazes me is not the event itself, but rather that I didn't mention it at the time. Not until what seems like ages after did it even cross my mind that cats don't do that! No one in the house owned a cat and neither did the neighbours, as far as I know. The living room windows were open, but there were no ladders, steps or nearby trees which a cat could have used to reach the windows.

In the month or so following, I met with a new girlfriend from out of town who came to visit briefly. Again, it was not until some time later that – during a phone call, I think – she disclosed she didn't know we had a white cat, whose presence she had inexplicably not brought to anyone's attention at the time of her sighting – which was odd, as she was a keen cat owner. She was unable to say where it came from or where it went. I can't even begin to speculate what took place, but that was no 'real' cat.

Ian MacKenzie, Birmingham, 2006

A Startling Memory Feat That *You* Can Do

"How I learned the secret in one evening. It has helped me every day."

When my old friend Richard Faulkner invited me to a dinner party at his house, I little thought it would be the direct means of doubling my salary in less than two years. Yet it was, and here is the way it all came about.

Towards the end of the evening things began to drag a bit as they often do at parties. Finally someone suggested the old idea of having everyone do a 'party-piece'. Some sang, others forced weird sounds out of the piano, recited, told stories and so on.

Then it came to Peter Brown's turn. He said he had a simple 'trick' which he hoped we would like. First he asked to be blindfolded. Those present were to call out 25 random numbers of three figures each, such as 161, 249, and so on. He asked me to list the numbers in order as they were called.

Peter then astounded everyone by repeating the entire list of 25 numbers backwards and forwards. Then he asked people to request numbers by their position in the list, such as the eighth number called, the fourth number and so on. Instantly he repeated back the correct number in the positions called. He did this with the entire list – over and over again without making a single mistake.

Then Peter asked someone to shuffle a deck of cards and call them out in order. Still blindfolded he instantly named the cards in their order backwards and forwards.

You may well imagine our amazement at Peter's remarkable memory feat.

"There was really nothing to it – simply a memory feat"

On the way home that evening I asked Peter Brown how it was done. He said there was really nothing to it — simply a memory feat. Anyone could develop a good memory, he said, by following a few simple rules. And then he told me exactly how to do it.

What Peter said I took to heart. In one evening I made remarkable strides towards improving my memory. In just a few days I learned to do exactly what he had done.

The most gratifying thing about the improvement of my memory was the remarkable way it helped me in business and in my social life. I discovered that my memory training had literally put a razor edge on my mind. My thinking had become clearer, quicker, keener. I was fast acquiring that mental grasp and alertness I had so often admired in men who were spoken of as "brilliant" and "geniuses".

Then I noticed a marked improvement in my writing and conversational powers. What's more my salary has increased dramatically.

"I can instantly recall anything I want to remember"

These are only a few of the hundreds of ways I have profited by my trained memory. No longer do I suffer the frustration of meeting people I know and not being able to recall their names. The moment I see someone I have met before a name leaps into my mind. Now I find it easy to recall everything I read. I can now master a subject in considerably less time than before. Price lists, reports, quotations, data of all kinds. I can recall in detail almost at will. I rarely make a mistake.

What Peter told me that eventful evening was this: "Send for details of Dr. Bruno Furst's Memory Course." I did. That was my first step in learning to do all the remarkable things I have told you about. In fact, I was so impressed that I got permission to publish Dr. Furst's Course myself.

My advice to you now is don't wait another minute. Full details of Dr. Furst's remarkable Course are available free on request. You could be amazed how a powerful memory can improve your opportunities at work and in your social life. You have everything to gain and nothing to lose by posting the coupon today.

BOB HEAP

We, the publishers, have printed full details of Dr. Furst's unique memory training method in a free information pack. For your free copy either phone our 24 hour enquiry line free on 0800 298 7070, post the coupon below (no stamp needed), visit our website at **www.firstclassmemory.com** or send an e-mail (see coupon). Or send your name and address to: Memory and Concentration Studies, FREEPOST VZM17T, Marple, Stockport, Cheshire SK6 6YA.

Apply for your copy **TODAY** and see how you could improve your memory.

To: Memory and Concentration Studies, FREEPOST FTM19 Marple, Stockport, Cheshire SK6 6YA.

Please send me your free memory information pack.

NAME...
Mr/Mrs/Miss/Ms.
ADDRESS...
....POSTCODE...................

POST TODAY, VISIT OUR WEBSITE AT
www.firstclassmemory.com
OR CALL 0800 298 7070 FREE QUOTING VZM17F
E-mail: VZM17E@firstclassmemory.com with your name and address

9 Wild Talents

There have always been stories of humans seemingly possessed of strange powers. While reports of telepathy and precognitive dreams are quite commonplace – and usually dismissed by the sceptics – what about first-hand accounts of levitation, passing through locked doors, or a modern-day Welsh witch who could apparently use her abilities to make mischief?

PRECOGNITION

PLEASE GENNY, CALL ME

When I was six years old, a woman who attended the same church told me that I was psychic. Luckily, the gift has always worked beneficially for me and although at the time it can be a little disconcerting, it has guided me through what could have been very difficult moments.

The most complex event was when my daughter, Genevieve, decided to fetch her husband from Heathrow airport when he was flying in from Frankfurt. They lived in Upton-upon-Severn, Worcestershire, only three miles (4.8km) from us, and as Gabrielle, her daughter of 15 months, had a heavy cold, she asked me to take care of her while she took their four-year-old son Daniel with her.

The early March day dawned clear and bright, though it was very frosty. I planned to give them lunch before they set out. As I was busy in the kitchen, I had a sudden vision. A freezing fog had come down and my daughter was involved in an accident on the motorway into Heathrow. It was so vivid that I felt all the distress as if it had already happened. I wanted to tell my husband, but there did not seem to be any point in both of us being worried.

My daughter arrived and I tried to persuade her not to go, without telling her why. Deep down I knew she would still go and I didn't want to chance precipitating the accident by putting the idea into her head. I argued that she should not leave her daughter when she was not well, but she laughed at the idea that Gabrielle would not be as safe with me as with her.

The sun was still shining brightly after lunch when Genny left for Heathrow and I stayed at home worrying. About two and a half hours later, the thick freezing fog came down. I tried to ring the airport but there was no reply – the fog had shut it down. The next four hours were the longest of my life – then the telephone rang. A London operator asked me to hold the line as she rang the number that had booked the call. A man answered and I heard the operator tell him that his call had come through.

"The young lady that booked the call went off to Birmingham in a taxi more than an hour ago" I heard him say. He told me what had happened. "The young lady was pulling off the motorway to go to the airport and braked behind the lorry in front of her. Her brakes failed. Somehow she managed to pull up by jamming on the handbrake and forcing the car into first gear, stopping with the car bonnet just under the tailboard of the lorry. I promise you she isn't hurt," he added quickly. "She didn't even seem shaken and the little boy is fine, too. There was a minute hole in the pipeline and the brake fluid had drained out on her journey. I have the car here at my garage for repair and she was told by the airport that her husband's plane has been diverted to Birmingham. She's on her way there now."

Soon, the telephone rang again. It was Genny's husband, Alan. "My plane has been diverted to Stansted," he said. "I have been trying to get through to Heathrow to tell Genny to wait for me at the information desk as I am arriving on the airport coach. Will you keep trying to get Heathrow and leave a message for her to stay where she is until I arrive?"

I explained that Genny was on her way to Birmingham. "You will have to get her by telepathy," said my down-to-earth son-in-law, "and tell her to return to Heathrow and wait for me there." I explained that I couldn't do that to order. "It's the only way," he answered. I settled down, closed my eyes and tried to imagine Genny on the motorway, thinking desperately, "Please Genny, wherever you are, telephone me."

Five minutes later, the telephone rang. I heard Genny's voice say without any preamble, "What's the matter Mum? I felt I had to phone you."

Later, I learned that on the way up to Birmingham, the taxi driver said he must

66 *I looked and saw a country lane lined with police cars and an ambulance* 99

stop at a motorway service station for cigarettes and as he pulled up Genny said, "I have to telephone my mother at once". It was only later that he found that his wife had put a packet of 200 in the glove compartment for him! They returned safely to Heathrow and Genny made her way to the information desk arriving at the same time as Alan.

Joan Weston, Leominster, Herefordshire, 1995

HE'S DEAD, HE'S DEAD!

In 1986, I was a student at North Staffordshire Polytechnic. On the night of 2 March, I had a disturbing dream. I was with a group of people in the country-side. Above me was an electricity pylon and along one of the cables leading from it a man was walking as if on a tightrope. Suddenly, the man slipped, fell across the wires and was electrocuted. To my right, a young woman walked past sobbing hysterically: "He's dead, he's dead!" I looked to my left and saw a country lane lined with police cars and an ambulance. The police officers came up to us and led us away one by one. As they came to lead me away I ran off looking for a tele-phone to call my father. I found one, but I couldn't get through. Then I woke up.

The following weekend, I travelled to Doncaster to visit my father. On the journey back, I caught a train from Doncaster to Sheffield, and as usual I sat right at the front of the first carriage. I regularly made the same journey, but this time was different. As I looked out of the window, I experienced fear and sadness and felt that I would never travel that route again. I reached Sheffield without mishap and left the train to find my connection to Manchester. It turned out to be the same train. I had a few minutes to wait, so I took a walk to steady my nerves. When I returned, I passed the replacement train driver as he was climbing into the cab. I remember looking at him and feeling sorry for him, but I couldn't explain why. I went to board the front carriage, to sit at the front as usual, but at the last minute changed my mind and moved back to the third.

The train had just reached the western side of the Pennines, outside a village called Chinley, when it crashed head on with a locomotive coming the other way. Fortunately we were travelling slowly after an earlier stop at a signal, but our driver was killed and there were many injuries, the worst of them being in the front carriage. When news of how bad it was reached my carriage, a young woman who was standing in the aisle to my right started crying and called out: "He's dead, the driver's dead!"

A few minutes later, the emergency services arrived along a country lane running alongside the railway on my left-hand side. They came onto the train and started to lead the injured off one by one. I was taken to hospital but soon released. My first thought was to ring my father, but I couldn't get through to him as he was making calls to find out if I was OK.
Paul Willoughby, Tottenham, London, 1997

SEA DREAM

In 1995, I was a deckhand in the motor-yacht industry in southern France. I was due to marry my fiancée, and that July I had undertaken a three-week trip that would help to pay for our wedding. On the second night at sea, our motor-yacht hit a violent storm in the Gulf de Lion. As an inexperienced seaman, I quickly discovered that I suffered from seasickness, which contributed to my falling violently on the aft deck. I bruised some ribs in the process and the captain quickly saw I was in no fit state to stay on deck. I was promptly sent to my cabin to rest, during which time I managed to catch about half an hour's sleep.

During my difficult slumber, I dreamt that I was in mortal danger and that I needed to see my fiancée. I vividly remember standing at the foot of our bed back home, watching over her as she slept. My dream was abruptly interrupted by the crashing of seawater penetrating the air duct above my head. I think for this reason I was able to recall this dream with such clarity. It was so real that the next day I recorded the time and date in my travel diary. The rest of the trip was very successful and I quickly explained my odd experience as a reaction to my first ever storm at sea.

Once reunited with my fiancée, almost immediately and without any prompting, she told me how on the second night I was away, she had been awakened by the silhouette of a man standing at the foot of her bed. She was terrified until she recognised the outline as my own. She thought the trip had been cancelled and that I had come home early, only to see the silhouette vanish! By checking my diary I was able to confirm the date and time of the event.
Eddie Grundy, Manchester, 2006

UNEARTHLY POWERS

A WELSH WITCH

In 1991, I joined my brothers Wayne and Geoff on a building job at the house of Mrs B—D— , whom they called "the Abergele Witch". They had worked for her before and the tales they told intrigued me.

We arrived at her small house, unloaded the van and went in. Wayne and Geoff introduced me as their younger brother Anthony and I shook hands with a normal, middle-aged woman with a pleasant smile. Introductions over, she went to the kitchen to make a cup of tea as we started to lay down the dustsheets in the hall where we were going to replaster the ceiling. Suddenly I heard Wayne swear. I was shocked to see him holding up a blood-soaked hand with a puzzled expression on his face.

"What the hell have you done?" Geoff asked.

"Nothing," Wayne answered. "It's just that I've got this damn wart on my finger and it's started bleeding."

We looked at each other oddly, then Geoff said: "You must have knocked it on the door frame or something."

I could tell by the look on Wayne's face that he hadn't knocked it at all. He went into the bathroom and washed his blood-soaked hand while Geoff went to the van for a box of plasters. I spotted some droplets of blood on the wall and wiped them off with a rag. My brothers rejoined me in the hall and we carried on preparing everything ready for plastering. Wayne's hand had now stopped bleeding, but the bravado and camaraderie we had displayed earlier had now vanished and we were now working in silence.

Mrs D— brought our tea into the hall and we all started talking to her about what colour paint she was going to put on the ceiling after it was plastered. Our conversation was eerily interrupted when water started to drip from the hall ceiling onto Geoff, who was sitting on the floor drinking his tea.

"Christ, what's that?" I said, desperately searching for one of the mixing buckets to catch the increasing flow of water.

After the initial half minute of bedlam, we asked Mrs D— where the main stopcock was and turned it off. Oddly, it didn't stop the water coming from the ceiling. It was then that I noticed the customer's totally calm demeanour. She didn't seem at all flustered or concerned about the leaky ceiling.

By brothers and I raced up the stairs and located the part of the floor on the landing directly above the leak, removed the carpet and busied ourselves pulling up the floorboards. After about 20 minutes, most of the landing floor was uncovered. We were astonished to find no water pipe in sight and everything under the floor bone-dry. When we went back downstairs there wasn't a trace of water damage on the ceiling. Wayne got the stepladder out and felt the ceiling where, only a short time before, water had been streaming into the bucket.

"Completely dry," he said.

Then we heard Mrs D— giggling from the other end of the hall. We replaced the floorboards and carpets, and plastered the ceiling as fast as humanly possible. We haven't worked for Mrs D— since.

Anthony Dorgan, Abergele, Clywd, 2000

THE LEVITATING HAMPER

At the age of 11, I was fascinated by the subject of the supernatural, reading everything I could find on the subject; I was particularly intrigued by accounts of children my age in whose presence objects flew across the room. I read that this was not an unknown phenomenon in youngsters on the brink of puberty and that in the Middle Ages children to whom this happened were considered to be witches and were buried alive, just for being the innocent victims of a poltergeist. While I was truly interested in this phenomenon, I was also truly frightened of it. I certainly never wanted it to happen to me.

One evening while taking a bath, I was luxuriating in the steaming hot water, the bubbles and the total relaxation after a hard day at school and hours of gruelling homework. My mind was a daydreamer's blank. I reclined in the bathtub facing a large metal clothes hamper. Fifteen minutes into my bath, the hamper slowly rose straight up at least two and a half feet (76cm) off the ground, momentarily paused suspended in mid-air, began to sway for several seconds, crashed down to the floor and began to violently rock from side to side.

My first impulse was to scream for my parents and run from the bathroom, but being exceptionally modest, I would rather have faced an unseen poltergeist than dash into the living room naked. My mother, attracted by all the noise, called up the stairs to inquire of its source. There was no way I could tell her that the clothes hamper just rose in the air. I would have been punished for lying. I just said "Oh, nothing", and stayed in the tub, by now too scared to leave it.

Then it happened again. This time the clothes hamper rose slightly, settled down with a shudder and began more subdued rocking than before. Enough was enough. I quickly rose, put on my pyjamas as fast as I could, and joined my family in the living room. I kept my heavy secret to myself.

To overcome my fear of our only bathroom, I tried to rationalise this happening as an inadvertent telekinetic occurrence brought on by my latent mental energy. My totally relaxed, tuned-out state didn't allow for the release of this energy, so it was directed to the only object in my direct view. Over and over, I made an effort to talk myself into this line of reasoning. After all, I had read a lot on the subject and this was a theory some scientists were offering – but in the far reaches of my mind I suspected a poltergeist was behind it. In time, my trepidation of the bathroom left, but I never again let my mind wander aimlessly while taking a bath. I told no one of the experience, neither friend nor family.

When I grew up and recalled the incident, I concluded that the rising of the clothes hamper was not the result of mental energy seeking an outlet but was the work of an unscrupulous spirit who harnessed that energy and used it to frighten a child through a telekinetic manifestation. No one understands why children, particularly girls on the verge of puberty, are the targets of these restless spirits. Even in children who are constantly being subjected to this phenomenon one finds that it tapers off or stops altogether with the onset of adolescence. I just know that as a result of my own experience many years ago I do not own a clothes hamper, and if I ever do get one it won't face the bathtub.
Connie van Hundertmark, Kew Gardens Hills, New York, 1982

AN ELECTRIC DIVORCE

It was not until our return from holiday in 1992 that my wife and I had any indication of discord in our daughter Charlotte's marriage. "I'm seriously thinking of leaving Charlie, I've told him that I am staying with you for a fortnight, to get myself sorted, one way or another!"

She was extremely unhappy – the vibrations oozed from her as if she were

" Strange occurrences began from the moment we arrived home "

radioactive. She was gifted (or cursed) with second sight, often describing visions she had seen as if they were actual happenings. Her ability to 'see' doesn't explain her latent knack for telekinesis. Strange occurrences began almost from the moment we arrived home.

Three framed silk plaques depicting animals shot across the room off the lounge wall, as if they had been thrown. Ten minutes after my wife replaced them, they shot across the room again. The radio-cassette wouldn't move from MW to FM; the selector refused to budge. I dismantled the radio and found the waveband bar bent. I straightened it, reassembled the set and it worked perfectly.

Charlotte missed her children sorely, telephoning them each morning before school and every evening before bedtime. David was 13 years old and Tina nine. Things always happened just after she had been on the phone talking to the children. The atmosphere in the flat was tense – occasionally we would hear the sound of sobbing from the bathroom. A picture frame fell from its hook on the wall. An ornament toppled over. The bulb in the refrigerator blew; the appliance was less than six months old. Charlotte was unable to get either BBC1 or BBC2 on the TV. Her mother or I would manage to get a picture eventually.

My wife found two figurines turned towards the wall and turned them back. The next morning they were facing the wall again. Everyone denied touching them. Charlotte had just put the telephone down from saying good night to the children. It was dark outside, so she walked over to the window and drew the curtains. As she did so, there was a loud 'plop'. One of the cluster of three spot lamps in the centre of the ceiling had blown. As we replaced the dead bulb, the one next to it failed and as that was replaced the third one blew.

One evening, there was a programme on the TV I wanted to record, but the video wouldn't work. Though it was an old set, it had never given bother before. Later, I learned that there was a trip switch at the back of the set. I reset it and the video worked as well as ever. The next morning, after Charlotte's phone call to the children, the microwave oven didn't work. After extensive trials, nothing could be found wrong with it. All the connections were renewed, it was cleaned and returned. It has worked perfectly since.

The fact that Charlotte was unaware of her power made the events seem even stranger. She decided to seek a divorce. She consulted her solicitor and they conferred for over an hour the next morning. When she came back, she was very depressed. The element burned out in the tumble drier and the automatic washing machine broke down. It was to be a week before the mechanic could fit us in and the pile of dirty clothes grew and grew.

Charlotte took a telephone call the next day. The answering machine made a bleeping noise and started flashing its light. It would no longer take and record messages. As the warranty had expired, more expense was in the offing. Our daughter's stay was not only fraying our nerves but costing us a fortune.

The last strange event was when Charlotte had finished talking to her solicitor on the phone. Her husband had made fresh demands regarding the settlement. As she came into the lounge, the clock on top of the television stopped.

Nothing has failed or moved on its own since the events catalogued here. Happiness has crept back into our daughter's life – she is divorced now, and lives in her own house. All the electrical appliances are working perfectly.
Bill McCarthy, Arboath, Angus, 1994

THROUGH THE DOOR
In 1958, I was enjoying my annual summer holiday with a handful of other children on a vast Kenyan cattle farm at Machakos, 40 miles (64km) from Nairobi, owned by a young English family. The eldest at 12, I had my own room, unlike the others who shared "dormitories". It was a small dressing room reached via the bathroom. The door between the bathroom and dressing room was the only way in and out, and the single window to the dressing room was heavily barred to prevent intruders. The farmhouse formed a large U-shaped bungalow around a central lawned courtyard. At that time there was no electricity on the farm, and lighting was by kerosene lamps.

One evening, we sat playing cards and telling ghost stories to frighten each other – which we did. I went to bed slightly jumpy, but after locking myself into the dressing room with the heavy 6in (15cm) long key, I soon fell asleep.

I awoke suddenly to see at the foot of the bed a figure, about 8ft (2.4m) tall, apparently draped in a beige sheet. It slowly and silently raised its arms from its sides, and in terror I leapt up and rushed from the room, yelling, my heart beating so hard and fast that it felt it would burst. As I raced across the courtyard, some adults charged out, the men with guns, the women shouting excitedly.

Breathlessly, I explained that there was a huge ghost in my room. This caused great amusement, and I was shepherded into the house, filled with cocoa and biscuits and a little tot of brandy, and assured that I'd had a nightmare. About an hour later, I had calmed down sufficiently and two of the women took me back to my room. The dressing room door was locked.

"Where's the key?" they asked.

"I haven't got it," I replied.

"Well you must have, because the door is locked."

"I didn't come out of that door," I answered, "I went through the other one."

"There isn't another door. You must have come through this one. Now what have you done with the key? Do you think you dropped it?"

I kept explaining that I hadn't stopped to unlock the door, and had run through the other door, but of course I knew there wasn't another door.

By the light of the kerosene lamp we searched high and low in the courtyard for the missing key, without success. The men were summoned, and using a piece of metal found the key still in the lock, inside the dressing room. It was carefully pushed out through the keyhole onto a sheet of cardboard and retrieved through the gap beneath the door.

We stood staring at the key, the adults amused and impressed by what they thought was a clever trick. I continued insisting that I had not come through the door, and soon their amusement turned to irritation. I couldn't have climbed through the window, because it was barred.

As we could all quite clearly see, the place where I said I had run from the room was occupied by a large wardrobe standing in front of a thick stone wall. For several days, the event was discussed with equal measures of amusement and irritation, as there was no rational explanation, and eventually the subject was dropped and faded. I have never since had any similar experience.

Susie Hiscock, St Romain en Charroux, France, 1997

10 *Weird Vehicles*

Phantom vehicles have long figured in the annals of ghostly encounters, from spectral stagecoaches to spooky sailing ships such as the *Flying Dutchman*. In more recent times, they've been joined by anomalous and anachronistic aircraft (sometimes whole squadrons of them), haunted digger trucks and a huge variety of bizarre and baffling cars and mystery motorcycles.

PHANTOM AIRCRAFT

NIGHT BOMBERS

The following happened when I had recently arrived back in the UK from New Zealand, so I estimate it took place about 1971. I was working as a chef in the village of Clare, Suffolk. Travelling home one night between 11.30pm and midnight, on the back road from Cavendish to Foxearth, (a very rural location), I became aware of a low droning sound. I stopped the car on a right hand curve, by a field, got out and stood on the edge of the field.

The night sky was filled with World War II bombers, I would guess I could see more than 30, flying spaced out, (I was not!) in the same direction and it was their prop engines producing the noise. I don't recall whether or not they showed any lights.

During World War II, this part of eastern England was peppered with airfields from where the bombing raids against Germany were launched. I believe what I saw was maybe one of the 1,000 bomber raids forming, which would have taken place maybe 30 or so years prior to my sighting. It goes without saying that by the 1970s there would only have been a handful of these planes still airworthy, and they would have been spread about around the world.

The fear of ridicule has meant that I have kept this largely to myself, but the utter strangeness of it has never left me, and I am now considering trying to recover this memory by consulting a medically qualified hypnotherapist, but they are thin on the ground here in Dubai where I live.

Finally, I was neither under the influence of alcohol or drugs, I am pretty level-headed and have not had any other inexplicable sightings before or since.

Glyn Jones, Dubai, United Arab Emirates, 2008

GHOST PATROL

In 1947, I was posted to Darwin, capital of the Northern Territory. Darwin was regarded as the gateway to Australia, and had suffered a considerable amount of damage by Japanese aircraft during World War II. In 1947, the population was around 6,000, so it was not crowded. There had been a large RAAF base, but most of the aircraft and personnel had been removed. However, there were still some operational aircraft that were frequently seen and heard, so that the sound or sight of an aircraft didn't arouse interest.

I was a member of the Quantas Airways ground staff, and there were about 100 of us living in converted army barracks nine miles (15km) out of Darwin. In those days, there was very little development other than in Darwin itself, and consequently I spent most of my off-duty time bush-walking and sketching the wildlife.

Some few weeks after I arrived, I was out in the bush when I heard an aircraft that sounded unusual. I cannot recall if it sounded laboured, was cutting out, or what the problem was, but it was sufficiently unusual that I stopped sketching and stood up to get a better look. The aircraft was flying at not much above tree height, and would pass almost directly overhead. It was a PBY Catalina flying boat like those that had been used extensively on coastal patrols during the war and had a well deserved reputation for reliability. As it passed overhead, I noticed two distinctly odd features: the port blister was armed with the gunner quite visible, his weapon at the ready, and the port engine was missing. When I say missing, I mean in the physical sense, not the electrical, as where the engine would normally be there was only a gaping hole. It was just as though the fitters had forgotten to reinstall an engine that had been removed for repairs.

The aircraft continued on its way and I eventually lost sight of it over the mangroves bordering a tidal inlet. I continued to hear it for quite some time after, until the sound eventually faded.

Over the next few months, I saw the same aircraft on probably a dozen

> **" He was sure no such aircraft was flying, and certainly not with one engine... "**

occasions, each time coming from the same direction, sometimes nearer to me than on others, but in every case, there was no mistaking that it was the same aircraft. By this time, I had become so used to seeing it that I knew the registration numbers, but time has erased these from my memory.

I must emphasise that I did not at any time regard viewing the aircraft as being odd, the only unusual aspect being that it was obviously on wartime readiness and that, for some reason, the technicians had not refitted the missing engine.

Then I happened to mention my sightings to a RAAF officer who was having a drink with us in the canteen. The subject came up only because we were talking about the relative reliability of various aircraft. The officer was at the time attached to RAAF Darwin and was familiar with all operational aircraft in the area. He was adamant that no such aircraft was currently flying, and certainly not one with only one engine. The subject must have intrigued him, for he contacted me some days later and confirmed that no aircraft of that registration was flying or operational within Australia. It was only then that I realised that I appeared to be the only person to have seen the craft, although a number of the staff were ex-RAAF personnel and naturally took more of an interest in aircraft than others who did not have that sort of background.

Following the discussion with the officer, I never saw or heard the aircraft again, although I was in the area for a couple more years. I am told by aircraft technicians that, although the Catalina had a good one-engine performance, this would hardly apply to take-off and continued operation, particularly where there was a great gaping hole which would cause monumental instability.

If I had seen the craft but once, it is probable that I could have been mistaken, but to see it frequently, and at close quarters, rather rules that out. I can but conclude that it was just another casualty of war, the difference being that this crew were determined to continue their patrol, at least until such time as they received recognition.

Mervyn FW Nightingale, Londonderry, New South Wales, 1998

CRASH VISION

One pleasant Sunday afternoon in the early autumn of 1941, my sister and I cycled quite a few miles north of Crosby, then a suburb of Liverpool, way past the Formby Point area, inland close to an RAF station. We had stopped on a rural lane amid conifers for a drink of tea from a thermos flask when we saw a twin radial-engined aircraft about 200ft (60m) above tree level. I was only 14, but knew all the aircraft types then flying, and identified it as an Anson. We saw that it was losing altitude at an alarming rate and I realised this was not an area suitable for landing. My sister pointed out there was no sound of an engine.

We cycled in the direction the plane had dropped out of sight. Leaving our bikes in a clearing, we ran through grass and bushes expecting to find aircraft wreckage strewn about; but there was nothing but quiet countryside. In any case, we had heard no noise of a crash. I remember a solitary seagull gliding silently by just as the enigmatic Anson had a few minutes earlier.

I haven't mentioned this episode to anyone until now. It was perplexing and outside normality (whatever that is). I am convinced that we had witnessed a spectral re-enactment or presentiment of an actual crash.

Mr DG Smith, Leicester, 2001

DRIVING ME CRAZY

HAUNTED DIGGER

One night, soon after I became a security guard, an excavator from a building site guarded by my firm was wrecked as it drove into a ravine. The guard said: "It just started up by itself and drove over the edge". Nobody believed him and he was summarily dismissed.

My firm and the site owners inferred that the guard attempted driving the machine himself for fun and had crashed it accidentally or deliberately, just to see the spectacle and relieve his boredom. If this were the case, I could not understand why he hadn't invented a more credible covering story; perhaps that intruders were to blame.

This incident was soon consigned to insurance company records, and for the next two years I continued to work for the security firm. I was assigned a permanent site guarding a compound and workshops owned by a demolition company, where lorries and heavy plant machinery were kept. I became friends with many of the drivers. When I arrived to begin a weekend shift one Friday in February, I was shocked to hear that a driver had committed suicide. He was a fervent, practising Spiritualist and had seemed to be a happy, easygoing man with a pleasant family.

The following Sunday evening at about 9:30, I was alone on the site in the security officer's cabin. The gates were locked and the 8ft (2.4m)-high steel spiked fence which surrounds the compound was a good deterrent to intruders. Looking out of the window, I noticed the orange warning beacon on top of a digger flashing 100 yards (90m) away across the compound. Going outside, I could hear the engine running.

I thought that either there were intruders on the site, or a mechanic had returned to work on the machine – although this seemed unlikely on a Sunday night. The gates were still locked and there was no sign of anyone on or near the machine. I left the digger running while I carried out a full patrol of the site looking for intruders or any signs of a break-in. I found nothing.

On my way back to the digger, a mere 20 yards (18m) off, its engine and flashing light suddenly stopped. Alone in the night, I felt a strange fear. For a moment I wondered whether I had imagined the whole incident, but the exhaust pipe was still hot. The ignition switch was off.

I stood in bewilderment, and was about to return to my cabin when the engine started up again! I climbed aboard again and with much jiggling of the ignition switch managed to stop the machine for good.

The following morning, I reported the incident to the compound manager and the mechanics responsible for plant maintenance. They told me it was impossible and asked how many bottles of whisky I had drunk beforehand. This light-hearted attitude was doubtless because no damage had occurred. If, however, the digger had been left parked in gear and started by itself, then it could have driven forward, destroying anything in its path and possibly wrecking itself. Is this what happened to my colleague who was sacked?

A sceptic might suggest that a short-circuit in the electrical system caused the machine to start up; but then it should have continued to run, since once started a diesel engine does not require the electrical system as long as fuel is supplied.

Could it perhaps have been the restless spirit of the recently deceased lorry driver trying to communicate?

Peter Eaglestone, Hexham. Northumberland, 1998

A MINOR OVERTAKING

In November 1963, I was driving from Cheltenham, Gloucestershire, to Chipping Norton, Oxfordshire, at about midnight. On a lonely part of the road that goes straight across the high Cotswold ridge, I was overtaken by a dark Morris Minor with its interior light switched on. The car seemed to be full of young people and, as the vehicle overtook me, they appeared to be moving about and laughing. It was a very strong impression. The car passed me at considerable speed, only to black out a few seconds later. I switched my lights to full-beam as I feared I would crash into them. Imagine my amazement when I saw a long empty road ahead of me. I tried to calculate whether they had been driving so fast that they were now out of sight, but this was impossible given the length of the road ahead and the duration of the overtaking.

The next day, I drove back along the route to see if there was any turn-off and discovered only the odd shut farm gate leading into a field.

Florence Jenner, Hurst Green, Sussex, 1997

UP TO THE BUMPER

My brother-in-law had an experience similar to that of Ms Jenner in 1995 while driving home to Berinsfield, just south of Oxford. He too was followed late at night by a car with its interior light switched on to reveal four occupants – although in this case they weren't "moving about and laughing", but sitting bolt upright in their seats, staring straight ahead like statues. The car was black and seemed oddly old-fashioned, although he wasn't able to tell the exact make or model.

It followed him in complete silence for several miles, accelerating and slowing down to ensure its speed matched his, finally overtaking at a junction only to vanish as suddenly and mysteriously as it had appeared. He still regards the experience as strange, disturbing and decidedly out of the ordinary. Berinsfield

isn't all that far from Chipping Norton where Ms Jenner's strange experience took place.
Dean James, Finningley, South Yorkshire, 1997

NIGHT RIDER
After reading the letters about phantom motorists around Gloucestershire and Oxfordshire, I will recount my own experience in the same area of the Cotswolds.

On 8 August 1997, I was stargazing with two friends, Kevin Donnelly and James Davies, at Ibssebridge near Bourton-on-the-Water in Gloucestershire. At about 1:30am, we noticed some strange lights in a field to the west. Thinking it could possibly be some late-night harvesting, we drove off to investigate.

We turned off the main road onto a much smaller road. After a short distance, a light appeared very suddenly in my rear view mirror. My two companions noted that it seemed to belong to an old-fashioned motorbike with a sidecar. Through the darkness (there were no street lights) it also seemed that the rider was wearing no helmet. The bike (or whatever it was) followed us closely and we were all agreed that something strange was going on. After what must have been about four minutes we came to a junction and the vehicle vanished. There was no indication that it had turned around as no tail-lights were visible. None of us saw the bike actually disappear – it was merely there one second and not there the next.

Somewhat perplexed, we eventually returned along the road to see if there was a simple explanation. As in Florence Jenner's encounter, there was the odd closed farm gate leading into a field that could not have been opened, driven through and closed without us seeing it happen.
Graham J Salisbury, Cheltenham, Gloucestershire, 1998

NUCLEAR NIGHTMARE
In the summer of 1985, I was living in rural Suffolk, and spent my university vacations working at a hotel near Woodbridge. At 11:30 one night in August or September, I was cycling the seven miles (11km) home through a very heavy mist with visibility down to about 20 yards (18m).

On the main Hollesley road, just before the front gate to the American air-force base, USAF Woodbridge, I suddenly saw, parked in the road in front of me, a large American car, dark in colour and with distinctive fins on the bodywork. The windows were either tinted dark or screened on the inside. It was so close

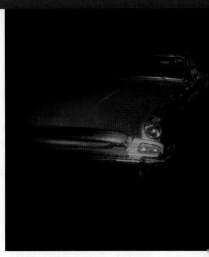

" It was a large American car, dark in colour and with fins on the bodywork "

that all I could do was brace myself for the impact and try to slow down so that, at best, I'd get away with a buckled front wheel.

Next moment, the car had gone and I was cycling on open road, still bracing myself for a collision. I cycled back towards Woodbridge for a couple of hundred yards, but there was nothing: no car, no turn-offs, and no gate access to the airbase apart from the main entrance. There was no "missing time"; I checked the time when I got home and my journey had taken me the usual time, about half an hour.

Had I slipped into microsleep on the ride home after a long day's work and experienced hypnagogic imagery in the mist? Had I called into being the situation I most dreaded? Or was it some sort of "objectification" of fears about the nuclear threat? It was at the height of the cruise missile furore and local rumour had it that USAF Woodbridge was storing undeclared nukes.
Paul Catlow, Stockport, Greater Manchester, 2000

GHOST CAR
When I was in college, I often had trouble sleeping and went for nocturnal drives. One night, I left the house at 11pm and drove through an old industrial area of Cincinnati. I noticed a white car behind me that I found disturbing. I drove on and it didn't follow, but a mile up the road I saw the same car, now facing me. I realised that what I found disturbing was that the car was plainly visible, but the headlights were off and looked black. I turned around to head home, but the car showed up behind me once more before I arrived. I thought

I had been out half an hour, but the clock showed 3am. I put the matter behind me until I read in an alien abduction book about lost time and people seeing things their minds couldn't accept and visualising them as owls or vehicles. While I don't buy the abduction business, the whole matter remains disturbing to me.

Walden Curtis, Cincinnati, Ohio, 2002

THE FLYING CAR

This puzzling event happened to my wife and me in the summer of 2001. We were travelling from our ranch in Texas to a business meeting in Kansas. I was driving our big, four-wheel-drive Ford crewcab truck about two hours before dark. Just north of the town of Aspermont, Texas, the road forks, and we turned right on Highway 87, a little-used stretch that runs straight north for about 35 miles (56km) to Guthrie, the next small town in this sparsely populated part of north Texas.

As I made the turn, there was a pale blue older model station wagon driving slowly ahead of me. I pulled out to pass and noticed the driver was a middle-aged woman with stringy blond hair, driving with her left arm on the open window, and wearing a stark white blouse. She continued to gaze intently straight ahead as we passed, which in itself was odd, since most people will look at a big black truck that roars by them on a deserted road doing 70mph (113km/h) while they are doing maybe 25mph (40km/h).

Some time later, we drove into Guthrie, having seen maybe two other vehicles along the way. Again, this was on a road that had run basically straight from Aspermont and was thus the shortest distance between those two points. After slowing down and going through town (there are no stop-lights), we accelerated in the open country beyond. Coming over a little rise, there was a very slow-moving vehicle a few hundred yards ahead of us. It was the same pale blue station wagon, with the same blonde driver wearing her white blouse, arm on the open window, and still going 25mph. I again passed her, but much slower this time, not believing what we were seeing. She didn't look at us this time either, even though I passed very slowly. How did she get ahead of me when we were driving nearly three times as fast over some 35 miles (56km) distance? I should add that this part of Texas has only the one paved highway going north, and there are no shortcuts. Somehow she got that little blue car to fly.

Grady F, Texas, 2004

ALL AT SEA

SHIPWRECK VISION

I saw something odd one clear day in March 1960 when I was working in a factory on the seafront at Portslade, East Sussex. The bell rang at 10am at the end of the tea break, and the workers made their way back to their machines. Before I followed them, I glanced out of the large windows.

As the canteen was on the top floor, there was a view of the harbour and far out to sea. The Brighton power station was across the harbour to the right. A large ship (probably a coal boat or similar) looked as if it has just left the harbour and was sailing towards Brighton.

I returned to work on the floor below, but something prompted me to take another look before I sat at my machine. Everyone else was busy, so it would have to be quick. The ship was now almost opposite the factory, having passed the power station, and I couldn't believe how far it had travelled. It still seemed to be moving at a great rate of knots when suddenly it appeared to stop dead. I lined it up with some nearby pylons and saw that it definitely wasn't moving.

It then tipped forward in slow motion, so that the bows were beneath the water and the stern was pointing skywards. The strangest detail was that the smoke, still billowing from the funnel, followed the deck-line, which by now appeared completely vertical. Within a few seconds, the whole ship made a nosedive and disappeared from view. By now I was in trouble for not being at my machine, and it was too late to ask anyone to confirm what I had seen.

The horizon was clearly visible and there were only a few tufts of cloud in the sky. Could I possibly have seen a reflection of a ship further out to sea? If so, how could I have seen the smoke billowing so clearly, and why would the ship have appeared vertical and not horizontal?

When my father returned home from his shift at the power station that night, I related my story. To my surprise, he didn't laugh but was very interested. He then told me the following.

He worked on the top floor at the power station and had a clear, uninterrupted view of the sea from Worthing to Brighton. The harbour entrance was very close by, and he knew that vessels kept their distance when they passed by the seaside of the power station.

On this particular morning, he was working quite close to a window that looked out to sea. As he glanced towards it, he saw the masts of a ship closer than he had ever seen one before. He felt certain that something was disastrously wrong and that the ship had surely gone aground. Making his machine safe, he hurried to take a closer look. He calculated roughly where the ship would be, but could find no sign of it.

We both agreed that the sky was clear and the horizon distinct. If it was a mirage, how could the size of the masts have taken up the whole view of the window where my father was working?

Rita Newman, Portslade, East Sussex, 2001

WAS IT *THE FLYING DUTCHMAN?*

At one point during World War II, I was on board a Liberty boat, the *James B. Francis*, in convoy from New Caledonia to the New Hebrides in the Pacific when a phantom sailing ship suddenly appeared late at night on our starboard side and parallel to us. It was very close and clearly defined; it stayed with us for about a minute, maybe less, then moved very quickly around to our stern and vanished.

It looked like a large sailing vessel with no sails at all, just rigging. It was lit from the deck up into the rigging, as if there were floodlights lying on deck shining straight up; the lower part of the vessel being invisible in the dark. The outline of the deck, the rigging and the masts were very visible against the black night sky.

The American crew dashed to their battle stations, but nothing appeared on radar. It would be interesting to see the ship's log: there were other vessels with

us, so the incident must have been well recorded.

Some years later, an article in *Reader's Digest* referred to the phantom ship I had seen as the *Flying Dutchman*; but the bright white "floodlights" differed from the description given by the 16-year-old Prince of Wales (later George V) in 1881 after his sighting: "At 4am the Flying Dutchman crossed our bows. A strange red light as of a phantom ship all aglow..."

Bill Lambie, Lower Hutt, New Zealand, 1995

When you see a building on one visit and it's completely vanished on the next, what are you supposed to think? Can bricks and mortar be sucked into another dimension? Or were they some kind of weird mirage to begin with? And then there are seemingly flesh-and-blood people who disappear before our very eyes, not to mention teddy bears abducted by aliens...

MISSING PERSONS

SPECTRAL SOCK SWIPER

In 1959, when I was 19 years old, I visited Alnwick in Northumberland to see a friend. One afternoon, at about 2.00pm, I was waiting for a bus in very bad weather, with thick snow everywhere. Standing to my right was an elderly lady. She wore a long black dress and shawl around her shoulders, her hair pulled back in a bun, her face very thin with deep, tired and sunken eyes.

She commented on the cold day and then asked me if she could have a couple of pairs of socks. It was only then that I noticed that her feet were bare. I took off my socks and handed them to her. She thanked me, put them on and as I stood there watching she simply vanished into thin air! Needless to say, my socks went with her.

I presumed she had died in or near that spot and that other people had seen her; perhaps many pairs of socks were now in her spirit possession. I was glad to help this poor unfortunate lady and maybe ease the pain of this earthbound soul. Throughout the encounter, she looked as real and as solid as a living human being.

Mrs VA Martin, Peterborough, Cambridgeshire, 1998

DISAPPEARING COWBOY

Around Christmas 1981, I travelled from Kentucky to California to spend the holidays with my family. When I arrived, the house was filled with the smell of food being prepared. I sat chatting with my eldest brother Pat. He brought me a glass of wine without asking me (I drink very little and never during the day), so I let the glass sit untouched. As soon as Pat settled in his chair with his glass of wine, my wineglass broke at the stem! No one was touching it. Pat swore and got up to get a towel. He was mad and mumbling something like "Leave us alone for a minute... it's my sister for God's sake..." I had no idea who he was talking to.

I picked up the glass and studied it while Pat got a towel. It was broken in an odd place; usually a wineglass will break at the narrowest part of the stem, or where the stem meets the base or the bowl. This glass was broken at the thickest part of the stem. I thought that was odd. While I studied my broken glass, Pat's glass, sitting on the table untouched, also broke, in the same odd place. Pat was livid. My sister-in-law seemed unsurprised. She mentioned to Pat that he should have known it would happen, after all "he" liked to break the good crystal. I asked Pat, "What does Kathy mean, you like to break the good crystal?" "Not me," he answered. I remained confused; no one was willing to explain to me that they knew the ranch to be haunted. During my stay that holiday, several more crystal glasses broke in the same way, always while the glass was untouched and in the same place on the stem.

My most frustrating experience at the ranch was on New Year's Eve. My family were having a party for their friends, most of whom were a lot older than myself. I was about 27 or 28 and most of the people attending the party were at least 40. I was the only single person, and I was bored. I had almost talked myself into getting a plate of food and going upstairs to start a new book, but stalled a bit. I thought there was still a chance I might meet an unattached young man, or at least, someone more in my age group.

I glanced at the fireplace – about 12ft (3.6m) from me – and noticed a young cowboy. An honest-to-God cowboy! He was wearing chaps, a cowboy hat hanging from leather ties around his throat, and spurs. What kind of person comes to a New Year's Eve party dressed as a cowboy? But then I remembered I *was* on a working ranch that still housed and tended horses, and maybe this guy had just finished work. It was only about 8 or 8:30pm. Anyway, he was my age and looked interesting. I wanted to talk with him. My plan was to stand where I was until he looked my way – but he never looked at me. He turned towards me, looked right

"What kind of person comes to a New Year's Eve party dressed as a cowboy?"

past me and turned to walk away. I followed him. He walked through the living room, dining room, and into the kitchen. There was a hallway off the kitchen with a bathroom. The door to the bathroom was standing open and he walked in. I decided I would wait for him. He didn't shut the door.

Another guest came from the other end of the hallway and started to swing the bathroom door shut so he could get past. He shut the door, took a couple of steps and decided to enter the bathroom himself. "Oh no," I said, "there's someone already in there!" He looked embarrassed and lightly tapped on the door. No one answered. He peeked in and found it empty. Yes, the bathroom did have a window, but it was only about 18in (46cm) wide and would have been impossible for a grown man wearing full chaps to have climbed through. Time would have been a problem as well. It was less than a minute from the time the cowboy entered the bathroom to the time the guest tapped on the door. Where did he go? I asked my sister-in-law, who was standing in the kitchen at the time, if she had seen him.

"A cowboy?" she asked. "Was he wearing chaps and spurs?" She could in fact describe him, but then said she hadn't seen him that night. None of the other guests had seen him either. I later learned that different family members had seen him on other occasions. There must have been 20–30 people at the party. I was the only one who saw the cowboy that night, and I had had only one drink.

After that New Year's Eve, my family told me that they suspected the ranch to be haunted. I couldn't believe it. The cowboy I saw was real, solid, not some gauzy, wispy thing. They agreed. One other apparition they witnessed, a sea captain from the 19th century, also seemed solid and real but could come and go in an instant. This would often be witnessed by two or three family members at the same time. Poltergeist activity was frequent and ranged from flying skillets to the shoving of family members.

Carla Griffin, Louisville, Kentucky, 2001

NOT FADE AWAY

My partner Anne and I had a very strange experience on 10 September 2005. We had gone shopping at Tesco in Prestwich, Manchester, and parked the car next to one of the glass shelters they keep the shopping-trolleys in. It was near closing time and the car park was virtually empty when we were putting the shopping in the back of the car. At this point, our attention was caught by a middle-aged woman pushing an empty trolley to the shelter we were next to.

What struck us about her was her strange expression. The best way I can describe it is the look people have when they have been humiliated but are trying to keep their dignity, so I assumed she'd maybe just come off worse in an argument with another shopper, perhaps over a parking space or something, but we had heard nothing and anyway, as I've said, the car park was practically deserted. The other strange thing was that she was facing forward, but seemed to be straining to look out of the corner of her eye to her right (more or less in our direction). As we tried discreetly to look at her, she just disappeared before our eyes – no fade out, no dissolve, she was just there one second and gone the next. The trolley, however, remained, rolling on under its own momentum for a second or two before suddenly accelerating and crashing into the other trolleys in the shelter.

I am at a complete loss to explain the events of that evening. I don't think we can employ the paradigm of the traditional ghost because there was nothing anachronistic about the woman (and let's face it – that *still* wouldn't be an explanation). As an aside, the Tesco in question is adjacent to a psychiatric hospital, and in fact is built on land once occupied by a chunk of that institution.

Barry Metcalfe, Higher Broughton, Greater Manchester, 2005

PHANTOM HILL-WALKER

On a beautiful sunny day about 10 years ago, my husband and I were enjoying a drive through the Berwyn Hills, North Wales, intending to have lunch in Corwen. As we descended the steep hill into Corwen, we both saw a tall, slim figure wearing a long, loose, russet-brown gown. He was striding smoothly and apparently without any effort up a rather steep, uncultivated, rough field to the left of the car. We were quite fascinated and slowed to a crawl. The figure crossed the narrow lane about 20yds (18m) in front of us, and seemed to completely ignore our presence. He then passed through a really thick hedge opposite.

We left the car and dashed down the road and over to the place in the hedge where he had vanished. We both noticed that the only other possible entry to this field was through an ancient and heavily barred gate that obviously hadn't been used for a long time. We scanned the field, but there was no sign of what we now assumed must have been a ghost.

We told our story at the inn in Corwen and the locals were very interested. One old gentleman recalled a story of a young priest who, long ago, had fallen in love with a young woman in what is now The Glyndwyr Hotel in Corwen. Their romantic secret was discovered and the priest vanished, never to be seen again. It was assumed that he met a nasty and grisly end. "Maybe you've seen his ghost," the old fellow said with a curious knowing gleam in his eye.
Josephine Treanor, Parkgate, Cheshire, 1996

CUDDLY ABDUCTEES

WAS TEDDY TAKEN?

I was born in a small surburban house in Southampton in 1963, and lived there until I was five. One of my earliest memories is of a teddy, which my parents seem to think was one of my third birthday presents.

I loved Teddy. He was just the best thing that had ever happened to me. One night I took him to bed as usual, and we fell asleep in our customary posture, with my thumb and forefinger firmly clasped around his neck. In the morning he was gone! I remember crying frantically, and the whole family helped strip my room in the search; but Teddy was nowhere to be found. I couldn't reach the window catch, nor could I have sleepwalked out of the front or back doors (both firmly locked) and left Teddy somewhere outside.

Teddy was replaced quickly, but 'Patch', in his pirate costume and the eye-wear which inspired his name, was never Teddy. I recently asked my parents about the episode. Mum and Dad remember the incident clearly, and admit to being as confused at the time as I still am now.

Is it possible that the Greys needed Teddy for some horrific experiment? Were they aiming for me and got confused? Was he ditched later? Did anyone find a surgically altered Teddy in 1967? Do any other readers have memories of missing toys? Was Teddy the only known soft toy abductee?

Simon Moss, London, 1997

The abduction of Simon Moss's Teddy might not be an isolated incident. I was a child of the Sixties too, and lived in south London. My teddy was also a firm and inseparable friend and I, too, awoke to find him gone. My parents were interrogated and everywhere was searched, but the teddy was not to be found. However, a few days later, first thing in the morning, he was found sitting in the spare bedroom in plain view to anyone entering the room. As in many alien abduction accounts, he was returned to the wrong location.

I now realise the possible implications of the bear's disappearance. I was too young to think of checking for unusual scars, implants or personality changes. Oh so many years subsequently passed while he suffered silently without counselling!

Sandra Bonnett, Christchurch, Dorset, 1997

Reading Simon Moss's letter about the vanishing bear brought to mind an incident in the mid-Fifties when I was about seven or eight. The bear in question was about 4in (10cm) tall, made of heavy pink plastic; the Daddy Bear in a set of three bear rattles given to my younger sister.

One evening, we were playing with the three bears and some other toys in the corner of the brightly lit living room. I had just gone across the room to fetch something and, as I came back, I accidentally kicked the Daddy Bear figure. It shot across the floor for about 18in (45cm), struck the wooden skirting board with a whack and promptly disappeared, never to be seen again, even though the whole family searched for it in what was quite a small room. I actually saw the toy hit the wall, and then it was gone.

Faced with something we couldn't explain, we simply ignored the peculiar little happening. Like Simon Moss, I can now only wonder if the Teddy was also an abductee.

Grace O'Halloran, County Cork, Eire, 1997

VANISHING CREAM

The abductions related by Simon Moss and Sandra Bonnett might not be isolated just to soft toys or to the Sixties. My incident happened in the early 1990s with tubes of E45 cream. My mother would buy this cream to soothe the eczema on my legs. It would seem that after only a few uses of the cream, the tube would disappear from its usual home in the cosmetics basket by the fireplace. Frequent searches around the house would prove fruitless, so another tube would be bought. Only upon the purchase of a new tube would the old one appear in its proper place.

Could it be that whoever took the teddies of Simon and Sandra are looking for a way to treat them from their scars of abuse (wear from affection)? Even more sinister is the possibility that Santa Claus is stealing people's medicines and selling them in poor countries – which I doubt!

Jamie Shilton, Berkshire, 1997

NOW YOU SEE IT...

DISAPPEARING HOUSE

In 1989 and 1990, I was living in Richmond, Indiana, while attending Ball State University in Muncie, Indiana, studying architecture. Three times a week, I would commute back and forth using US Highway 35. About halfway between the two cities is the small town of Economy. Just east of there, on the south side of the road, were the remains of an old farm. The barn was still there but the house had been torn down. However, because five or six trees were still standing on the lot, I could tell where the house had been.

Because of my interest in buildings, I was curious about the house that had been there. In the fall of 1990, I moved back to my hometown in northern Indiana. The next spring, I was taking a trip to Columbus, Ohio, and decided to go that route even though it was longer, because I needed to pick up a transcript from Ball State on the way. As it worked out, I was travelling through Economy about 8:30 that night. I stopped in town to put the top up on my Jeep and continued on. As I passed the farm, I was excited to see that someone had built a house on the lot where the old house had been. The windows were lit up, although the curtains were drawn so I couldn't see inside.

It was very simple – a basic rectangular shape, front door in the middle, two windows on either side, five windows along the second floor, very close to what I would have assumed to be there originally. No outside lights on. As I was running late, I continued on and didn't think much more about it. On Sunday afternoon, I was returning home the same way and, approaching the farm, I was glad that it was daytime so that I would be able to see more of the house.

However, as I got closer, I realised that there was no house on the lot; just the barn and the trees. I'm very sure I wasn't dreaming or imagining the house as I had just stopped to put my top up (not an automatic one, I had to get out and physically put it up) and was wide awake.

Herb Bailey, by email, 2003

ROAD TO RUIN

In March, I started running a new route that takes in a mile-long boreen (small country road) linking two bigger roads. About half way along this boreen is an old two-storey house, after which my route becomes more of a dirt track that is hardly, if ever, used these days. In one of the fields behind the two-storey house is a plot of land in which the bodies of unbaptised babies used to be buried. There are numerous such graveyards in this part of east Mayo (in Ireland). I knew at the outset that this plot contains the twin of a relative of mine who is now in his mid-eighties. He maintains that the track is haunted and will have nothing to do with it. I also know that the plot is now marked officially in some way and lies on the right-hand side of the track, but I don't know its exact location.

Anyway, on my second or third run up the track I was on the lookout for any potential gravestones or other signs when I noticed a derelict, two storey, stone-built house in a field, also on the right-hand side of the track. It must have been an impressive building in its day and quite a rarity too: I know of only two other houses of a similar age and size in this part of the county. However, the only parts left standing now are the two end-walls, both heavily overgrown with ivy.

The next time I did the same run, two or three days later, there was no derelict house or any evidence of one ever having stood near the track. Since then, I have done the same run 20 or 30 times and surveyed the surrounding countryside from every possible angle. Nothing. Furthermore, when I asked my relative about the house, he was adamant that to his knowledge there had never been any such building on that track.

Sean Ottewell, Ballyhaunis, County Mayo, Ireland, 2006

There's no clear-cut boundary between the waking world of consensus reality and the realm of dreams, but there's a vague, in-between territory, which we might call the "Twilight Zone". Here, a Polish icon grows an extra scar, as do all its reproductions; overnight, a fish tank is drained and a bathroom spattered with blood-like stains; and an invisible something is peeing in the saucepans...

WHILE YOU WERE SLEEPING...

BLOODY BATHROOM

On 1 January 2005, my partner Barrie and I woke up to find the floor of our bathroom covered in clots of blood. A quick, panicky check showed that neither of us was, or had been, bleeding, and that the 'blood' was in fact something else. It was slightly sticky and dark red – like blackcurrant cordial – and had no smell. It reminded me in colour and texture of dark red lip-gloss; but I don't use lip-gloss, and I'm fairly sure Barrie doesn't either.

We had been out the night before and come home at about 3.30am, each of us using the bathroom before retiring. Although we had been celebrating New Year, neither of us was so drunk as to have been unable to miss the Grand Guignol effect, which was quite impressive. As the bathroom is very small and the splats fairly close together, we would have been bound to step in them had they been there when we got home. The splats had not been trodden in and the soles of our shoes were clean. There was no direction to the splats, such as you'd get if you shook, say, a tube of ink with the top off. Instead they looked like the effect you get when several large drops of rain hit a pavement: evenly distributed over the floor, but missing the bath, basin, loo and shelving.

Unfortunately, Barrie cleaned up the 'blood' while I was looking for my

camera, so I can't show you what it looked like. We still can't think of a logical explanation; it seems that sometime between 3.30am and 10.30am on New Year's Day, our bathroom was the scene of an extremely localised 'shower of blood' effect – but I've never heard of one of these happening indoors.
Sarah Walker, Norwich, Norfolk, 2005

RIPPING YARN

One night in the autumn of 2001, I went upstairs to bed and took off my blue jeans and T-shirt, leaving them folded up on the bed in the spare room. The following morning, I found the crotch and seat of the jeans had been ripped with such ferocity that they were completely ruined. At first I blamed my neighbour's cat, but the animal was not in the house. I live alone, and there was no one else in the house. I can't explain it as alcohol-induced memory lapse as I had not been drinking.

Had I ripped the jeans in my sleep? If so, how? Bare hands couldn't have done the damage, as the tears were not down the seams; besides, I have no history of this type of behaviour. Perhaps an eccentric housebreaker with a grudge against jeans (and the thoughtfulness to lock up afterwards) or a phantom clawed creature was responsible. I have not experienced anything similar before or since, but I take care now to hang up my clothes in the wardrobe just in case.
Nick Appleton, Castleford, West Yorkshire, 2003

ADDAMS FAMILY VANDALISM

In 1965, I was obsessed with the *Addams Family* TV show. As a child of 10, I watched the programme closely, making notes, as I constructed a cardboard replica (pictured page 153) of the Addams Family's haunted house. I tried to duplicate all the details of the house, such as Morticia's famous wicker chair and the stuffed two-headed turtle.

The next year, we moved into a new home, close by in the same town of Canoga Park, California. One of the first possessions I took to our new home was my highly prized model Addams Family house. One day soon after we moved in, only my mother and I were home and I was in my room looking at my cardboard haunted house that was placed on a card table, when my mother called me for lunch. In less than an hour, I came back to my room to find the haunted house positioned on the floor next to the table.

Everything was torn up in the model as if an angry little demon had gone wild

" Everything was torn up as if an angry little demon had gone wild in the model "

in it. Items that were glued on the first floor of the model had somehow ended up on the third floor. The strangest thing was that several plastic ghosts that I had glued throughout the model were all gone – never to be found again! It was as if something was enraged by the little plastic ghosts and had torn them all out. It was really perplexing, seeing that only my mother and I were home and she would never destroy something I made – she always appreciated the creative things that I constructed. The only conclusion I can come to is that some unknown entity had spirited away the little spooks. I still have the Addams Family house and what happened to it remains a mystery to this day.
Jeffrey Vallance, Reseda, California, 2006

FISHY MYSTERY
On 14 September 2001, my girlfriend and I and our one-year-old boy were staying with my brother Paul in Brisbane, Australia. I turned in at about 1am, while my brother stayed up till about 2am watching football. I awoke from a bad dream at about 3am, which is very uncommon for me. At the same moment, our boy had also awoken, and was crying for a feed. As I was very used to waking up in the middle of the night, I felt quite alert, and walking through the lounge to the kitchen I noticed nothing out of the ordinary. Our boy next woke up at 6am, so I got up with him and went to the adjacent lounge to veg out to early morning kids' TV. It was early spring, and, feeling the chill, I checked to see if the windows had been closed the night before – they had.

Next to the TV was a small 12 x 6 x 6in (30 x 15 x 15cm) fish tank on top of a large, old stereo speaker. I think I was just staring blankly at it when I realised that it appeared to have been emptied. My first thought was that somehow it must have sprung a leak. On close inspection, I saw that the tank had been emptied save for the bottom inch (3cm) of water, and weirdly the little goldfish was swimming in a sea shell at the bottom of the tank, which contained just enough water to hold the fish. I couldn't see a single drop of water on the floor around the tank or in the speaker box. Later, we refilled the tank and to this day no leak has occurred.

Where did the water go? As mentioned, it was cool in the house with all the windows closed. When my brother awoke, I filled him in on this little mystery much to his complete bafflement, and being a scientist he set out to solve it. Two years later, we're still scratching our heads. The best scenario we could come up with is that it may have been some kind of bizarre prank, but I strongly doubt that anyone would have gained entry to the house without at least waking me, because the front steps and wooden floor creak very loudly, the walls are thin, and I'm a light sleeper. Today the same goldfish swims happily in the same tank.
Michael Metcalfe, Melbourne, Australia, 2003

ANOMALOUS IMAGES

CUT-UP MADONNA
The following event was witnessed by the whole population of Poland, where I used to live. It's amazing that the Catholic Church, to the best of my knowledge, appears to have remained silent about it. It happened sometime between 1982 and 1985. As you probably know, Poland is an intensely Catholic country, and the monastery on Jasna Gora (Bright/Luminous Mountain) is the centre of worship, a kind of Polish Mecca.

The monastery houses the most venerated religious icon in Poland, the 14th-century painting of the Virgin Mary, the so-called Black Madonna of Czestochowa. The picture hangs on the wall of almost every Polish home. Its most noticeable and best known characteristic is the two long and vaguely parallel scars that run across the right cheek of the Virgin. Legend has it they were sword or lance cuts made by the Hussites who in the 15th century stormed the monastery and were trying to destroy all religious images.

Then suddenly, literally overnight, those scars elongated; previously they ended at the jaw, but now they crossed the whole cheek and extended onto the neck. This has happened not only on the painting itself (which would be possible to explain as a case of vandalism or some natural fault slowly becoming apparent) but also on every photograph of the painting, of which there must have been millions in circulation.

My father was then working as a county architect in Wieliczka near Cracow, in which capacity he knew a good number of locals. One of them was a woman who owned a little private store (a thing that was still extremely rare in those Communist days) with all the religious paraphernalia: crucifixes, books, pictures etc. It was she who told my father that when she came in the morning to open the shop, she was astonished to find that all the images of the Black Madonna in the store now showed the elongated scars. That's how I found out about the story.

As soon as my father came home from work we went through all the photographs of the icon we had at home, both as pictures on the walls and in coffee-table-type books, and we discovered that what the woman said was indeed the case. It was more than spooky. It was easy to see where the old scars ended and the new additions started, because the new parts were bright red, like fresh wounds (I kid you not). With time, they acquired the same brownish colour as the old ones.

While we (and, I suppose, millions of other Poles) were perplexed, we still tried to find some rational explanation, mostly along the lines: "Maybe it was there all along, but we just didn't notice". Alas, that explanation was easy to discount; my father used to paint a lot as a teenager, and one of the paintings we still had in my grandparents' house in the country was his replica of the Black Madonna painting. At the first possible occasion, we drove to the country house where we discovered that on my father's painting the scars were still short as they used to be and as we all remembered them.

It seems that the change occurred only on the icon itself (the most closely guarded painting in the whole of Poland) and on all the photographs of it, but not on any paintings etc., that were not exact replicas of it. As I was just over 10 years old then, I can't really remember what the reaction of other people was, or whether there was any official statement by the Church.

However, I very well remember the actual event, and in my humble opinion it makes any other allegedly miraculous occurrence, be it Fàtima or Lourdes, seem like a non-event; here we have an observable phenomenon that left material traces and was witnessed by millions of people and can indeed still be seen today. In my mind there are only three possible explanations as things like hoax or mass illusion can safely be discounted:

a) Some sort of collective national consciousness was at work, doing a bit of psychokinesis. The era was particularly interesting: it happened around the time of the 600th anniversary of bringing the icon to Poland and around the time of Pope John Paul II's second pilgrimage to his homeland; it was also not very long after the martial law and suppression of "Solidarity". Some researchers might argue that during times like these some kind of super-consciousness can manifest itself in the material world.

b) There's a Cosmic Joker, or some kind of alien intelligence that likes to make jokes of this type at our expense.

c) Or it's a genuine miracle in the sense ascribed to that word by Christianity.

I'm still as perplexed by it as I was all those years ago.
Arthur Chrenkoff, Brisbane, Queensland, 1996

BLESSED BUM

A strange image (pictured page 157) appeared on a canvas chair in our kitchen in April 1997. Neither the bottom nor the jeans were an obvious match for anyone in our household and we were at a loss to explain it. Friends dubbed it "the arse rubbing of Totnes" and it became something of a magnet, a shrine almost, for people fascinated by the unexplained. Comparisons with the Turin Shroud – though absurd – were inevitable, and people were not slow to theorise. Hypotheses ranged from the far-fetched ("The chair is haunted by the bottom of a former user") to the even further-fetched ("A burglar suffering from 'bottom dandruff' broke in, sat in the chair, and left without stealing anything.")

A local healer suggested that "just as crop circles are a message from planet

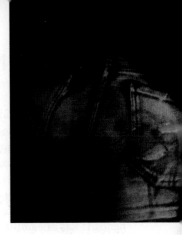

> **" Opinions differed as to the gender of the bottom. Most men tended to see it as female. "**

Earth to its out-of-touch, brain-limited antennæ – humans – so might the 'rubbing' be a message from the root or base chakra, represented by the bottom, to the airy 'heady' atmosphere of our home, exhorting us to become more in touch with the processes of nature, of the body, of the *material* world." Could be – it's as good a theory as any. Sneerers and sceptics suggested that someone in the house dusted his or her bottom with flour or talcum powder and then sat in the chair – but both of us swore this wasn't so and, more tellingly, all efforts to replicate the image in this way failed.

Opinions varied as to the gender of the bottom. Most men tended to see it as female, while most women tended to see it as male. We allowed people to sit on the "rubbing" for a small fee and had some surprising feedback. Reports of relief from minor ailments were not uncommon. These included rashes, runny nose, tickly throat, sore wrist, etc, all of which might have cleared up on their own. Less numerous but nonetheless regular were claims, subsequent to sitting on the "rubbing", of significant weight loss from hips and thighs. One individual reported spontaneous remission of hæmorrhoids; a majority reported feelings of increased wellbeing, clarity of purpose and internal security.

I must confess to having experienced none of these benefits myself and make no claims whatsoever for the image – save that I found it æsthetically pleasing, an interesting talking point and a small but welcome source of revenue. I'd be interested to know if anyone else has encountered similar images, or if they can come up with any more satisfying and feasible theories than those given above.
Matthew Harvey, Totnes, Devon, 1998

JUST PLAIN WEIRD

FEATHERED TIME SLIP

In 1978, I lived in Royston, about 12 miles (19km) south of Cambridge. One night, I set out on the five-minute walk to the Royston Royal British Legion for a drink. The commercial break in Coronation Street was just starting, which would make it about 7.40pm. I walked past the railway station and turned into a short-cut through a small housing estate for the elderly. At the back of one of the buildings there was a lawn and I noticed a large barn owl sitting on the back of a garden bench. It was a beautiful bird and as I was only a few feet away I stopped so as not to scare it; but it showed no sign of fear and sat looking back at me. It did not stir when I walked past it.

When I got to the Legion Club and ordered my drink, I was very surprised indeed to see that it was 9.20pm. I had not stopped to admire the owl for that long and I was sure I had no feeling of vagueness or having been asleep.

The next day, I went back to the lawn to see where I had come across the bird, but the bench was not there. There was a bench on the lawn, but it was at the far end, a good 20–30ft (6–9m) away and was set in concrete and overgrown with weeds.

Chris Precious, Dover, Kent, 1996

BURIED MINCE PIES

Since about 1968, my parents lived on the outskirts of Leicestershire, near the village of Anstey. My father built a garage at the bottom of the garden in the early 1970s, and shortly afterwards a slim conifer (I think that they are called skyrocket) was planted near the back door of the garage. It grew to the height of around 7ft (2m).

After my father died in 1994, my mother became concerned that someone could hide behind the tree and pounce on her coming out of the garage. We all recognised that this was unlikely, but nevertheless decided to dig the tree up. One early summer afternoon, I began to dig around the roots and rock the tree to loosen it from its 'moorings'. As the roots gradually emerged, three very pale white objects appeared from amidst the roots. The surface soil was clear – conifers, of course, don't permit other plants to grow beneath their leaves.

The objects, which at first I took to be some sort of fungus, came easily away from the roots and the more we looked at them the more we thought that they

looked like home-made mince pies. We broke one open to reveal mincemeat. They appeared 'fresh', although the pastry was very pale. We were surprised to find them since we could see no reason for them to be there and the ground had generally been undisturbed for the best part of 25 years. We kept the pies in the freezer for some years afterwards finally disposing of them when my mother moved to a smaller house.

David Knight, By email, 2002

PHANTOM PIDDLER

Some years ago, urine kept appearing in covered pans and casseroles in our house, and also flooded the cooker at various times. We owned no pets then. The suggestion was that it could be from a badger or large hedgehog – either of which I am pretty sure I would have noticed. The phenomenon stopped after about a year, which was a great relief to me as I was spending a fortune on disinfectants and bleaches. It wasn't ever on the floor, but always in containers; the frying pan was a favourite repository.

Goodness knows what was responsible – I am just thankful it has gone away. Odd happenings abound in this old house, but we can cope with them, just as long as the phantom piddler keeps away.

Roz Wolseley-Charles, Malvern, Worcestershire, 1997

STAR JELLY

The following incident happened in the late 1920s when I was eight or nine. I was reared on a mountain farm in County Antrim in Northern Ireland and, being a bit of a loner, I would wander through the fields searching for the nests of skylark, curlew and the like, and exploring fish-life in a small stream that flowed through our land.

One day in a rough grazing field I came upon two hemispherical mounds of a translucent, whitish jelly, about the size of large upturned bowls, separated by about 10 yards (9m). I remember that they wobbled when I touched them. I then – stupidly, in retrospect – inadvertently put a finger to my lips. The taste was very acidic. The childish thought that struck me was that they had come from the stars. At that time in our part of the country, profound sages were thin on the ground and no one was interested. I did mention the occurrence in an English composition at my local school, but I cannot recall any scientific interest being aroused. I returned to the spot a few days later, and had trouble finding two faint circles on the ground. The memory of finding these objects is still vivid after all these years.

TS Gore, Belfast, Northern Ireland, 1997

Fortean Times would like to thank all those who have written to us to share their experiences over the past 36 years. A particular thank you goes to those writers whose letters appear in this volume:

Edwin Airey, Garrick Alder, Nick Appleton, Barbara Ashton, Herb Bailey, Ken Baron, W Ritchie Benedict, David Bent, Michael Billing, Claire Blamey, Sandra Bonnett, Colin Bower, Christine Bretherton, Kate Brett, Paul Brooke, Valerie Button, Graeme Cammack, Denny Casely, Paul Catlow, Roz Wolseley-Charles, Arthur Chrenkoff, Tony Clark, Raymond J Conduit, David Cotton, Walden Curtis, Roy Dent, Anthony Dorgan, Peter Eaglestone, Robert Evans, Grady F, Maggie Southam Ferrari, David Fideler, Mario Fiorillo, Amy Ford, W Ford, Alan Gardiner, Bill Gibbons, Mrs Sandy Gibson, Richard Gipps, Stella Maria Goddard, TS Gore, Paul Graham, Carla Griffin, Rob Grimes, Eddie Grundy, Mrs M Gunn, Chris Halliday, Anthony Hampton, Matthew Harvey, Rachel Hazard, Victoria Rice-Heaps, PJ Heaton, Brian Henson, Susie Hiscock, Anthea Holland, Paul Hughes, Helen Humphrey, Connie van Hundertmark, Dean James, Florence Jenner, Glyn Jones, Ian Kidd, David Knight, Ken Lake, Bill Lambie, Mrs PE Laver, Steve Leggett, H Leigh, Judith Lunny, Ian MacKenzie, Tim Marczenko, Mrs VA Martin, Bill McCarthy, Annie McEwan, Jennifer McGhee, Barry Metcalfe, Michael Metcalfe, Dr Rufus S Morgan, Simon Moss, Susi Mulligan, Mazda Munn, Rita Newman, Mervyn FW Nightingale, Grace O'Halloran, Sean Ottewell, Trevor Ouellette, Graham Oxley, Edwin Page, Chris Peers, Rhonda L Perry, Ian T Peters, Travis Pitts, Ida Pollock, Chris Precious, Alan Price, Simon and Effy Price, Benjamin Radford, Jonathan Ratty, Martyn J Renton, Jeff Revis, Phoenix Rhiannon, John F Rice, Ben Robins, Zvi Ron, David T St Albans, Graham J Salisbury, Julia Morgan-Scott, Andrew Shilcock, Jamie Shilton, Mark Sidwells, Paul Sieveking, Bart Smith Jr, Mr DG Smith, Alex Solari, Mark Spurlock, Jeff Stevens, Mr GE Thompson, Richard Tomkinson, Susan Topping, Elaine Towns, Josephine Treanor, Jeffrey Vallance, Sarah Walker, Michael Walton, Mark Warner, Joan Weston, RB Williams, Jake Willott, Paul Willoughby

Thank you to those who helped make the pictures in this volume happen : Abigail, Paul Cooper, Kate Cornish, Capucine Deslouis, Alex Godfrey, Rebecca Jezzard, Lapin.

FOR MORE REAL-LIFE STORIES OF THE UNEXPLAINED, SIGN UP TO THE *FORTEAN TIMES* MESSAGE BOARD AT WWW.FORTEANTIMES.COM/FORUM AND VISIT THE 'IT HAPPENED TO ME!' FORUM.

IF YOU HAVE YOUR OWN BIZARRE STORIES TO TELL AND WOULD LIKE TO SHARE THEM WITH US, THEN SEND YOUR LETTERS TO: PO BOX 2409, LONDON NW5 4NP, UNITED KINGDOM, OR EMAIL SIEVEKING@FORTEANTIMES.COM